The History of Fishing
TABLE ROCK LAKE

Tom Koob
6/07

by Tom Koob

I

Printed by
Litho Printers
Cassville, Missouri

WHITE OAK LODGE PUBLISHING

HCR 1, Box 4089
Shell Knob, MO 65747

cover design by Bob Bruffett

Second Printing - 2007

INTRODUCTION

I wrote this book for three reasons: I love history, I love fishing and I love Table Rock Lake. For several years, I've heard stories about the area and lake; what fishing was like before the lake, what the lake and fishing was like in the early years, what's buried beneath Table Rock's waters and how the project was built.

As I began to research information for this work, I was repeatedly told that many of those who knew the stories weren't around any more. I realized that it was important to document some of this information before it was lost.

I have tried to make this book entertaining, interesting and factual. My research combined scientific studies, literature review, personal interviews and my own experience. I am indebted to those who supplied information, especially the Missouri Department of Conservation employees who did the bulk of the scientific studies on Table Rock and its fisheries. I also want to thank all those who agreed to share their personal stories in interviews.

Many others including my wife and family, fellow anglers, those who supplied photos, librarians, my printer and manuscript reviewers were helpful and patient in supporting my attempt.

I hope you enjoy this book. I hope it gives a clear picture of the history of this wonderful resource, Table Rock Lake. I also hope you can use it as a reference for specific facts about the lake.

Keep the water clean.

Tom Koob

Chapter 1
Early History

The White River valley has been a fishing area for millions of years. During the geologic Ordovician period 435 to 500 million years ago, this area was covered by a shallow sea. The many fossils of small sea creatures found in the Ozarks' rocks are testimony to the life and death of many types of aquatic animals and fishes. Certainly, these fishes were part of a vast food chain, wherein larger fish ate smaller fish. This is the way nature has played out for millions of years.

Eventually, the land rose and the sea drained. Forces of erosion created the deep gullies, ravines, hollows and valleys of the Ozark region. Water carved the rock and formed the many streams and rivers of present day northern Arkansas and southern Missouri.

The White River rises as a spring in Arkansas' Boston Mountains near St. Paul. It flows generally north entering Missouri where it takes a primarily eastward course before turning south back into Arkansas. The White then follows a meandering course basically south and southeast before emptying into the Mississippi just above the mouth of the Arkansas.

The portion of the White River impounded by Table Rock Lake has three major tributaries: the James River from the north and the Kings River and Long Creek from the south. This portion of the river also has many streams, creeks and springs.

Archaeologic evidence indicates native Americans inhabited the White River valley about 10-12,000 years ago. Indian campsites and villages were almost always located near good water sources. These early inhabitants were primarily hunter/gatherers, but they undoubtably took advantage of the available fishery. Numerous fish bones have been unearthed in bluff shelters. Ancient bone fish-hooks and fragments of nets have been found in this area. It is probable that several means of fishing were used including spearing, trapping and netting. It is interesting to imagine the same spear points that were used to kill mastodons and giant sloths may have also been used to take sturgeon or largemouth bass. There is also good evidence that Indians of this area used ground mussel shells in their pottery.

The native Americans that lived in this area were isolated from more advanced cultures like the Hopewell or Mississippian groups. By the Woodland period (1000BC-1250AD), native peoples in the White River valley had acquired bows and arrows. These people were the Ozarks Bluff Dwellers and often inhabited the large overhanging cliff recesses of this area. Prior to Table Rock Lake forming, a bluff dwelling near Golden, Missouri was found to contain numerous artifacts including human and animal bones, pottery and arrowheads.

Other evidence of Indian presence during the Woodland Period has been discovered in cairns on Philibert Bluff, at the confluence of Long Creek and the White and the Loftin site where the James meets the White. In 1954, the Corps of Engineers contracted the University of Missouri to perform archaeological salvage projects in areas to be flooded by Table Rock Lake. In 1957, the University of Arkansas Museum in Fayetteville began digs on sites in Arkansas that would be inundated by the lake.

Around 1250AD the Indian peoples called Ni-U-Ko'n-Sha or Children of the Middle Waters inhabited the upper White River basin. This group, the Osage, were an impressive people of large stature, fine features and great endurance. The Osage were the first Indians to have contact with white settlers in this area. Following a treaty between the Osage and the United States government in 1808, other eastern native Americans moved into this area. From 1821 to 1833, Indian trading posts existed on the White River at Swan Creek, Turkey Creek and near the mouth of the James. In late 1837, the Cherokees on their forced relocation passed near Flat Creek on the infamous Trail of Tears.

Prior to the Louisiana Purchase of 1803, white settlers to the White River valley were mostly trappers. Due to the ruggedness and poor soil of this region, it was slow to attract pioneers. The river itself though has always been attractive to settlers. The rivers and streams of this area not only provided water, but also transportation and a food source. Undoubtably, the early pioneers of this river basin fished the waters for food.

Steamboats and flatboats plied the White River from the early 1800's. The river was a major, though difficult source of transportation for goods and people into the Ozarks and for shipping products like railroad ties out of the region. According to Goodspeed's 1888 History of Barry County,[1] "In 1851-52 the county granted some money to be expended on improving the navigation of White River.... During the session of the Legislature in 1854-55 a bill was introduced by Senator John Gullet from this district, the title of which was "A Bill for the Improvement of the Navigation of White River," asking an appropriation of $10,000 out of the state treasury;...that sum was expended on said river." Apparently, these efforts were only partially successful. In 1859, the steamboat Ray reached the mouth of the James River, the farthest point ever reached on the White River by steamboat.

In the latter part of the nineteenth century, lumbering became widespread in the White River area. The pine forests were almost completely logged out. Oak and cedar were also extensively logged. Often this cut timber was shipped out of the area by floating huge tie rafts down the rivers to processing plants. Goodspeed[2] wrote "On June 3 (1874) Francis James and Jack Leonard of the Shell Knob neighborhood, started from the mouth of Kings River with a raft of cedar eighty yards long and twenty-two yards wide. Since 1874 rafting has not been unknown here."

Stories are told of some brave anglers who fished from these tie rafts. An angler could ride the raft and fish different locations. If he found a good pool, he would walk along the raft and continue to fish the same area. Good balance was required.

Much of the timber cut in the White River region was for railroad ties. The development of railroads in this area had a significant impact. The rails brought people and money into the Ozark hills and were responsible to a large extent for the growth of towns like Branson, Hollister and Reeds Spring. Ultimately, the railroads made this region more accessible to sportsmen and started the growth of tourism. One interesting effect of the logging industry came from a Missouri Supreme Court ruling in Elder v. Delcour. This case found that all Missouri streams are open to canoeing and fishing because they are navigable waters by warrant of their use to float ties.

The lumber industry also had a negative impact in the White River Valley. Removal of the native trees eventually led to a different type of landscape. The pines were replaced by oak and cedar. Large areas of clear cutting contributed to increased soil erosion and area flooding.

In 1897, a large pearl was discovered in a mussel shell by Dr. J.H. Meyers on Black River in northern Arkansas. When news of this find spread, people began collecting mussel shells from the area rivers in large quantities, hoping to find pearls. These pearls brought prices of a few cents to several hundred dollars each, depending on size, shape, color and luster. By 1900, collecting freshwater mussel shells for buttons was also found to be profitable. Tons of shells were gathered and shipped down the White River on flatboats. It took about 40 bushels of shells to make one bushel of buttons. Eventually, portable button extractors were used on the upper White to saw out the blank buttons at the site of harvesting. This industry which provided a decent supplemental income to the White River residents continued until about 1940.

Since the first time man walked along its shores, the White River has provided water, transportation, income and food. It has always been an integral resource and inspirational fountain-head to the area's inhabitants.

Chapter 2
Fishing the Rivers

During the first half of the 20th century, the rivers and streams that would become Table Rock Lake provided a rich fishery for the rugged people living in the area. Many local people never owned a rod and reel, but fish they did. Wading or using wooden boats, they seined minnows from the small streams to use as bait. The minnows native to Ozarks' streams include the gizzard or hickory shad, bleeding shiner, Ozark minnow and horneyhead chub. Several types of darters are also indigenous to the White River watershed.

Trot lines were the preferred method of catching fish. There was no restriction on the number of hooks used other than what an angler owned or the length of his line. Trot lines were run across the rivers from shore to shore or tied up on one shore and attached to a rock on the other end which was dropped mid-stream. These folks didn't have a lot of leisure time, so lines were often set and checked at night or on Sundays.

Bob Philibert of Shell Knob tells a story about trot lining. He and a friend took out one evening on the White with their gear and a johnboat. They beached their boat on shore, set a trot line and camped for the night. Overnight, a heavy storm blew in and the river rose dramatically. Philibert said the rising water washed away the boat and his pants. He reported he never got the boat back, but he did find his trousers.

Limb lines and hand lines were also frequently used. Many local fellows carried a hand line with them. If they were near the river with a little time on their hands, all they had to do was catch a grasshopper, bait their hand line and pitch it out into the water.

Catfish, drum, bass and carp were often taken using these methods.

In the 1940's, J.D. Fletcher fished the upper White River around Eagle Rock and Shell Knob. Using homemade tackle, J.D. and his father would head out to areas like Deer Bluff or Big Creek. One of his earliest fishing outfits consisted of a pole cut from a hazelnut tree, thread from a flour sack for line, a hook made from a bent straight pin and a metal nut for weight. They had several methods for obtaining live bait. One involved driving a heavy stake into the ground to scare up worms. They also seined minnows in Roaring River and Big Creek. A favorite catfish bait was rabbit entrails. J.D. recalls catching mostly catfish and drum.

Another early fishing technique used was gigging. One type of gig consists of a wooden pole about three feet long with one to five barbed metal tines at the end. Wading or floating in a john-boat, a gigger could 'spear' fish like carp and suckers. J.D. Fletcher of Golden recalls using a gig with a much longer handle, up to 12 feet long. A long length of cord was attached to the end

A 20 pound catfish from the James river, early 2oth century.

of the handle and looped around the gigger's arm. This type of gig was actually thrown like a harpoon and required considerable skill. Buster Tilden of Galena gigged suckers, catfish and walleye from a johnboat in the James.

Gigging was often done at night from a boat. Early anglers would attach pine knot torches to the bow or side of their johnboats for light. On July 16, 1896 near the mouth of Indian Creek, Albert Pitts gigged a 101 pound catfish.[3]

A catfish caught from Taneycomo in the early 20th century.

Joe Kuklinski with catfish trotlined below Taneycomo in the 1950's.

J.D. Fletcher with a boat load of gigged carp. Note long handled gig.

Noodling or hand grabbing was also practiced. Noodlers would scout out submerged hollow logs in the rivers or set their own. They would also 'feel out' hollows or openings along the banks. This method required the 'grabber' to wade up to the cavity quietly. He would reach up into the hole and feel for a fish. If he found one, he would carefully place his hand inside the fish's mouth or gills and grab ahold. The fight would then be on as the grabber attempted to pull the fish out and haul it to shore or into the boat. Some noodlers employed hay hooks or short gigs instead of a bare hand. Large catfish were most often taken using this method.

Local residents of the White River valley fished primarily for food. Fishing was a fun and cheap way to put food on the table. Most fish were eaten fresh, but some were canned. Suckers especially could be cleaned, pressure cooked and then preserved in Mason jars. Sucker grabbing continues to this day as a method for catching large numbers of fish, particularly in the spring.

Prior to the lakes, suckers were usually taken with gigs. Today, they are caught during the spring in the area creeks and rivers. Sucker grabbing refers to a unique angling method. A sucker grabber uses a very short fishing rod or sometimes just a rod handle. A stout line or cord with a fairly large weighted treble hook is attached. The grabber stations himself in the stream on foot or on a step ladder for better visibility. Some brave grabbers climb into overhanging trees or limbs along the shoreline. Others fish from horseback. Where there are long shoals, a method of 'herding' suckers may be used. One person stations himself at the foot of the shoal and throws rocks into the water, 'herding' the fish upstream to a waiting grabber. Sucker grabbing is essentially sight fishing in which the angler is attempting to snag visible suckers.

Nixa, Mo. has held its Sucker Days each May since 1955. Founded by Finis Gold, this event attracts thousands of visitors to the Nixa area. Each year, starting in March, area anglers head out to the local streams and rivers like the James, Finley and Swan Creek. The best grabbin' for white, yellow and redhorse suckers is in the shoals when the water is fairly high and the weather warm.

The fish are brought into Nixa where they are scaled, filleted, scored to breakup small bones, coated in special corn meal mix and deep fried. The flavorful fish will often feed three to five thousand people. In recent years, lower creel limits, low water levels and fewer fish have reduced the total take of suckers for this event. Nevertheless, Nixa continues to honor this tradition and supplements the fish fry with store-bought fillets as needed. In addition to feeding lots of folks, Sucker Days provides several charitable donations. The streams and rivers of the Table Rock Lake area continue to provide a source of enjoyment and food today, much as they did decades ago.

Fish traps were used in the streams of the White River valley for years. Small traps consisted of a mesh container with a funnel at one or both ends. The trap was baited and sunk in a pool. Early traps were woven from thin oak strips. Later, wire traps were used.

Shoal-type fish traps required considerable construction. A small dam was built at the foot of a shoal. Several poles were laid horizontally and placed about 2 inches apart below the dam. The outer edge of this pole rack was raised slightly. Fish would flow over the dam and become trapped on the poles. Large numbers of fish were taken with this method until it was outlawed around the turn of the century. Ingenthron[4] relates a story about a shoal-type fish trap constructed at Cedar Point shoal under what is now Lake Taneycomo. This trap provided considerable food for the local populace during the drought year of 1901. In the early 1900's, the town of Cape Fair is reported to have used a large seine net stretched across the James River to capture large numbers of fish for a hungry citizenry.

Wallace Lea, presently of Powersite, Missouri, grew up near the Finley River in the 20's and 30's. He remembers making many fishing trips to the stream. He would cut his own pole from a tree, tie on some linen line and a hook. Using live bait like minnows, crawfish or worms, he caught largemouth, smallmouth and goggle-eye (rock bass). Wallace often fished from the shore, but also used a boat made of two hoods from a Hudson welded together. He also used a wooden boat hand-made by his father.

The rivers and streams of the White River valley have long been known for their clarity and cleanliness. However, anywhere there has been concentrations of people or animals, these waters have been susceptible to pollution. As early as the 1930's, concerns about contaminated Ozark waterways have been raised. K.C. Sullivan, PhD. State Plant Commissioner and Entomologist completed a study for the Missouri State Game and Fish Department in 1933.[5] He studied the aquatic animal life in the James River as an indicator of water quality. The following is an except from his report:

"These streams of the Ozark region are ideal for most of the game fishes, particularly bass, perch, crappie and catfish, and in some cases trout.

Due to the lack of adequate protection in years past, and to the present popularity of the region as a tourist and summer resort, the problem of keeping the streams adequately stocked with fish is a serious one. However, the State Game and Fish Department is making rapid progress, and in so far as means will permit, is making a preliminary biological survey of the more important streams.

During the summer of 1930, a preliminary survey of a portion of James River, in Christian and Stone Counties, probably the best bass stream in the middle west...was made. This work was carried on under the direct supervision of G.M. Kirby, Chief of Hatcheries of the Missouri State Game and Fish Department.

The reason for selecting these streams was due to the fact that James River in its tortuous course passes near Springfield, Missouri, a city containing nearly 70,000 people, and a considerable portion of the material from a sewage disposal plant finds its way into the river, through a tributary, Wilson Creek.

Considerable complaint from sportsmen had been received by the State Game and Fish Department that the sewage coming into these streams was killing fish.

Summer floats are a very popular diversion on most of the larger Ozark streams. In making these floats, a boat from sixteen to eighteen feet long and three to four feet wide, called "John-boats" is used. The necessary equipment and supplies are stacked in the center of the boat. A guide with a strong paddle, steers from the rear end. The front end is utilized as a place from which to fish. The nights are spent on suitable gravel bars."

Dr. Sullivan goes on to describe the numerous small aquatic organisms he found in the James River and Wilson Creek. Although methodology and specific data results were not listed in this report, he goes on to make some conclusions.

"The riffles of James River are rich with aquatic life, there is abundant food to support many more fishes than are now present in the river. From the great quantity of aquatic life encountered, it seemed evident that the material from the sewage reduction plant, at Springfield entering through Wilson Creek, has little or no detrimental effect upon life in James River.

Evidently, the scarcity of fishes is due primarily to the intensive fishing which has been carried on. With adequate protection, the fishing on James River should again become as good as it was in years past."

It appears that Dr. Sullivan believed that pollution was not a problem at that time and that fisheries, at least in the James River, could be better maintained by stocking programs or fishing restrictions. As the years passed, interest in controlling water pollution as well as more restrictive fishing regulations would gain considerable support.

Just as Roaring River flows along its course and eventually becomes part of Table Rock Lake, the history of Roaring River is an integral part of Table Rock's story. The Roaring River spring area was settled in the early 19th century and served as a power source for mills as well as a fishery. Goodspeed[6] described the area as follows: "Roaring River rises in a fathomless spring. This is an even flowing well far back in a grotto, whence the waters flow and spread out into a lake. Prior to 1880 a dam was constructed at this point level with the spring. Before the construction of this dam, the waters rushed from the grotto down the rocks with a sound and splash which merited for the stream its name. The lake is a favorite haunt of delicious fish, speckled trout twelve inches long being caught there."

In 1905, Roland M. Brunner purchased the spring area and developed it into a resort. He built a hotel and some cabins and stocked the river with trout from a hatchery he built just below the spring. His development didn't go as well as expected and was eventually offered in a foreclosure sale.

Dr. Thomas M. Sayman purchased the 2400 acre parcel on the Barry County courthouse steps on November 16, 1928. Within three weeks, he donated the property to the state of Missouri. Missouri designated the area Roaring River State Park. During the 1930's, the state and especially the CCC (Civilian Conservation Corps) did extensive development in the park. Many of the buildings, trails and other improvements completed by the CCC are still in use today. During this period, there were two lakes at Roaring River. The upper lake developed by Brunner was washed out in a flood in 1938. The lower "bass lake" was built by the CCC in 1936. It existed until the state drained it in the 60's. Remnants of the lower dam can still be seen today toward the lower end of the park.

Roaring River has been operated as a trout park and hatchery since the early 1930's. Opening day March 1st has always been a very popular event. The excellent trout fishery attracts anglers from around the world. Roaring River has been responsible for luring many visitors to this area. In addition to the clear, cold water this stream contributes to Table Rock, it also acts as a source for rainbow and brown trout. The stream is stocked with about 200,000 trout each year, about half of those raised in the Roaring River hatchery. Some trout released in the park eventually make their way to the reservoir and become part of Table Rock's fishery.

Devil's Pool is one of the geologic oddities of the Ozarks that contribute to the natural beauty and historic lore of the Table Rock Lake area. Located in Big Cedar Hollow just above Long Creek, Devil's Pool was a clear, cold spring emanating from a cleft in the rock walls of the valley.

The native Americans of the area considered the spring a sacred pool with healing powers. Early settlers in the region deemed the pool "bottomless" and wondered at the white, blind fish it contained. They named the mysterious, secluded spring Devil's Pool. In the 1920's, Harry Worman and Jude Simmons bought the acreage around the site. They both built beautiful summer homes on the property and had a road built to their residences. Although neither Worman or Simmons were serious outdoorsmen, they and their guests did occasionally fish Big Cedar and Long Creek during their stays at the summer retreat.

Worman divorced his young wife Dorothy in 1935. Dorothy later died under mysterious circumstances. Her body was cremated and H. Graham Clark, founder of the School of the Ozarks, scattered her ashes into Devil's Pool. The vacation homes were seldom used after Dorothy's death and the property was eventually purchased by a logging company. The land was clearcut which led to erosion and spoilage of the spring.

Dan Norris bought the Devil's Pool land in 1947 and attempted to restore the spring with limited success. Norris did develop the property considerably turning it into Devil's Pool Resort. He built cabins, a swimming pool, horse trails and remodeled the Worman and Simmons houses.

Devil's Pool Ranch operated as a resort and dude ranch throughout the fifties. When Table Rock came in, the resort became a popular destination for fishermen. A dock was built and fishing boats were supplied. Several area guides worked out of Devil's Pool including Charlie Campbell. The resort was operated under various owners until 1964.

After 1964, the beautiful Devil's Pool area languished, mostly unused and neglected. Johnny Morris, founder of Bass Pro Shop, purchased the property in 1987. He extensively developed the area, restored the original homes and created Big Cedar Lodge. Today, this first class resort attracts vacationers and anglers from throughout the country. There are still reports of ghostly images seen on the property- perhaps Dorothy Worman seeking peace at Devil's Pool.

The springs, streams and rivers of the White River Valley have provided fishing and recreation for centuries. During the last several decades, fishing traditions developed that still influence the way we approach these waters and their fisheries.

Chapter 3
Float Trips

Float trips started in the Ozarks around the turn of the century. Visitors to the area's spas and springs were attracted by the many fine float streams and the great fishing. The event that probably first widely publicized float fishing in the Ozarks was an excursion on the Current River organized for Missouri Governor Herbert S. Hadley in 1909. A photograph of the party at Round Spring was widely publicized and drew national attention to the sport and this area.

Harold Bell Wright the author of The Shepherd of the Hills made at least two float trips in the early 1900's. One from Galena to Branson of about a week and another of two weeks. He apparently did little fishing, but may have received some inspiration for his well known books.[7]

Charlie Barnes of Galena is usually credited with creating the first johnboat. He modified a gigging boat by shortening and widening it. The boats were mostly built from pine, but redwood and cedar were also used when available. These craft were 20 feet long and about 30 inches wide. Some boats used on the upper White were narrower.

Charlie, Herb and John Barnes established the Galena Boat Company, the area's first commercial float fishing operation. In addition to building boats, they guided five day trips on the James and White River from Galena to Branson. Charlie later built boats and also guided for Owen Boat Line.

Jim Owen owner of the Owen Boat Line out of Branson, Missouri is probably most responsible for publicizing and popularizing float fishing on the upper White River. Starting in the 30's,

Owen ran floats almost daily on the James, upper White, Kings and Buffalo Rivers. Floats could start near Galena on the James or Eagle Rock, Shell Knob or Radical(at Hwy. 13) on the White.

The Owen Boat Line primarily catered to affluent anglers from cities of the midwest, but also guided many celebrities of the era. These anglers were serious fishermen and used the best tackle of the day. Most fished with casting rods and baitcaster reels like Shakespeare, Langley and Pfleuger. They used artificial lures like the BassOreno, Peck's Bait, Lazy Ike, Flatfish, River Runt and Hawaiian Wiggler. These fishermen (and sometimes women) caught lots of smallmouth and largemouth bass. They also took goggle-eye, catfish, walleye (jack salmon) and even eels.

Owen's johnboats were built by Charlie Barnes of Galena. They were made of pine with metal ribs, usually with a seat in the back for the guide. Clients sat in deck chairs placed in the boats. Some of these craft had a false bottom to keep equipment and feet dry. These floats were always guided by a local man who worked for a daily rate and tips. The guide steered the johnboat with a wooden paddle. They also set up camp, cooked and gave fishing advice. Many float trips included a commissary boat.

In the days before the big reservoirs, float trips lasted several days. Many floats would end at Taneycomo, but some continued down the White into Arkansas. At the end of a trip, boats and equipment were shipped back to Branson and Galena by truck or railroad.

Buster Tilden of Galena was a guide for Jim Owen in the 40's and 50's. He floated many trips on the James and White and some on the Buffalo in Arkansas. Some of his floats started as high up the James as the mouth of the Finley. Others started several miles up Flat Creek. Many of these trips ended on Taneycomo where the guide would often use a small outboard to make the final run into Branson. Some guides would stay over in Branson at Owen's bunkhouse.

Buster's guiding started in May when the stream bass season opened and ran into the fall. He floated with clients from all over the country including Springfieldians Ralph Foster and Bill Ring of KWTO radio. Most of these anglers used good quality equipment. Shakespeare and Pfleuger baitcasting reels on aluminum, steel or fiberglass rods were common. A few liked to fly fish for bream.

Others enjoyed trot lining at night. Many guides discouraged trot lining due to the extra work involved. When live bait was desired, glass minnow traps were placed in the stream to acquire baitfish. Most of the float anglers used artificial lures like the Crippled Minnow, SOS or Peck's Bait. Tilden's biggest bass, a 7 pound largemouth came out of the James on a Peck's Bait. He relates a story about this large horsehair jig with a small spinner attached at the head. One of Buster's fellow guides liked to drink. On one occasion, this guide told his clients that they'd have to give him a snort of their liquor every time they got hung up. The prideful anglers took up the challenge and then proceeded to take their guide's advice to fish a Peck's Bait really slow. The heavy, large-hook lure provided several shots for the guide that day.

The float guide's day was a long one involving loading equipment, steering the johnboat, giving fishing advice, cooking meals and setting up camps. Larger floats often had a commissary boat hauling equipment and supplies. The commissary man would float ahead of the others and set up the lunch and overnight camps on gravel bars. There were many established camps along the river routes. In addition to the guide and angler clients, the johnboats carried wooden camp boxes, ice boxes with large blocks of ice, tackle, food and water jugs. Guides were typically paid $4-$5 a day plus tips.

The fishing in these streams was for largemouth and smallmouth bass, walleye, catfish and suckers. Fish were often eaten on the trip, but seldom taken home.

Buster Tilden fondly remembers his days on the river before Table Rock. He is proud that he only sunk his johnboat once. Flat Creek was a fast flowing stream and Buster was guiding a client who had only one leg. Trying to push his boat past a snag, the johnboat turned sideways and filled with water. His client only lost his lunch and a couple of bottles of beer, but he was hopping mad.

The first half of the 20th century saw extensive float fishing in the upper White River basin. In addition to the Barnes' and Owen's operations, Bill Rogers and Lyle Chamberlain outfitted float fishing excursions. Other names associated with the industry were Yocum, Long, Stewart, Dillard, Hemphill and Melton. For several years, Galena was known as the "Float Capital of the World". Float fishing had a sizable economic impact on the area through employment and the sale of goods. It attracted visitors from all over the country including movie stars, politicians and national sports writers. The enjoyment and fishing success these clients experienced added to the considerable popularity of the upper White River basin as a desirable destination for angling and vacationing.

GALENA BOAT COMPANY

DENNIE LONG, Owner and Manager

Phone 45 · · · · · · · Galena, Missouri

We furnish the following equipment for Float Trips on the James and White Rivers

ALL ITEMS OF EQUIPMENT ARE LISTED BY THE DAY

EQUIPMENT	PRICE	TOTAL
____Boats, per day _____	$2.00	$_____
____Tents _____	1.50	_____
____Cots, each _____	.50	
____Chairs, each_____	.50	_____
____Cook Outfits _____	1.00 up	_____
____Tarps _____	.50	
____Minnow Traps_____	.50	_____
____Buckets_____	.25	
____Thermos Jugs_____	.25	_____
____Thermos Coolers_____	.50	_____
____Bed Rolls_____	1.00	_____
____Ice and Grub Box _____	.25	_____
____Car Storage_____	.50	_____
____Guides_____	7.00	_____
____Beer_____	____	_____
____Groceries_____	____	_____
____Driving Cars _____	____	_____
____Transporting Boats_____	____	_____
____Miscellaneous_____	____	_____

Galena Boat Company price list early 1950's

After Bull Shoals was completed in 1951, floats were primarily on the James and upper White above Branson. When Table Rock was finished in 1958, the era of the big float trips began to wane. Some outfitters continued to operate on the upper James while others like J.D. Fletcher floated the White and Kings in Arkansas.

Larry Bunch of Galena began fishing the James River area about the time Table Rock went in. He fished and guided float trips on the James in the mid-60's. Table Rock had shortened the practical distance for floating to one half or one day floats. The river had also changed from natural processes and human development. The banks eroded and large trees fell into the stream. Pools silted in or filled with gravel. New channels were carved. Despite these changes, the remaining float services clung to the old ways. Larry guided for Bill Rogers earning about $20 a day plus tips during the summer, the primary float season.

Owen's float guides, 1939. l. to r. Claud Williams, Jake Benhand, Little Hoss Jennings, David Barnes, Tom Yocum, Theodore Barnes, Al Cunard, Glenn Henderson

They still paddled 20' wooden johnboats like the ones Charlie Barnes made 30 years before. Wealthy clients from the midwest area fished for largemouth and smallmouth bass, goggle eye, crappie and catfish. Many older lures like the Midge Oreno and River Runt were still used, although newer baits like the Rooster Tail and Rapala were also employed. During the 60's, Larry's clients had good tackle using Ambassador baitcasters and fiberglass rods. Others began to fish with spinning outfits and closed-faced reels like the Zebco. A few would flyfish. A few would stillfish with live bait.

Owen float party meal. Tom Yocum upper left. Note table supported by cot and water jug.

J.D. Fletcher in one of his johnboats in the early 1960's on the upper White before Beaver.

By the end of the 60's, the float fishing business on the James was nearly extinct. Many of the clients had migrated to the big lakes. The wooden johnboats were briefly replaced with fiberglass models and then aluminum canoes. Larry Bunch fondly remembers catching a 5 1/2 lb. Kentucky bass floating the James. He is proud to have been a part of the float fishing era, even at its end.

Although there are still serious anglers floating the tributaries of Table Rock, the big lakes changed the float business forever. The streams have changed from erosion, siltation and pollution. Most outfitters today use aluminum canoes and cater to large groups of young people, youth groups and organized parties. The partying drifters far outnumber the fishermen.

J.D. Fletcher bought two wooden johnboats and the gear to go with them from Rube Dick in 1959 for $200. These boats were built locally out of pine or ash and were very heavy. The seams were tarred, but they still leaked. J.D. organized float trips on the upper White. These were typically one day floats starting at Lost Bridge (just above the present site of Beaver Dam). They made their way on down to Hwy. 62 and Beaver Town before completing the float at Eagle Rock.

These trips were organized for people who liked to fish. Customers were charged $22 a day for two people. J.D.'s early clients used tackle like South Bend and Shakespeare baitcasters with braided line on steel or plastic rods. Plugs like the Creek Chub Pikie or Heddon Lucky 13 were used to tempt smallmouth and largemouth bass. One of Fletcher's guides hand carved a cedar bait called an Ozark Ike and sold them to customers for a dollar each.

When Beaver Lake was completed in 1964, J.D. moved most of his floats to the Kings River. These trips usually started at Trigger Gap at Hwy. 221 and ran downstream to take-out points at 62 Hwy., Grandview, Summers Ford and Smith's Landing just above the Arkansas line. Fishing tackle was developing dramatically during the 60's. Anglers began using spincast outfits like the Zebco and Johnson with fiberglass rods and monofilament line. This type of tackle was inexpensive and allowed even inexperienced fishermen to cast smaller, lighter baits like the Midge Oreno, Lazy Ike and plastic worms. These baits were well suited to float fishing for

21

smallmouth and most of Fletcher's customers caught lots of fish. In the 70's, Fletcher's Guide Service started using 14 ft. aluminum johnboats. Tackle continued to develop with anglers using sophisticated baitcasters, spinning outfits and graphite rods and occasionally fly fishing gear. Lures like the Bomber, buzzbait and jig-and-pig were being used to take quality catches of black bass, white bass and walleye.

As angling became more technologically advanced and fishing pressure increased on Table Rock during the last two decades of the 20th century, Fletcher's Ozark Float Fishing provided an alternative to fast-paced bass fishing. His float trips continue to offer an excellent way to relax and enjoy quality fishing.

J.D. is a master at serving his clients and promoting his business. Over the years, he has guided many famous media names, local personalities, politicians, entertainers, athletes and sportsmen. His clients include Jim Owen, Ralph Foster, Smiley Burnett, Bill Ring, Harold Ensley, Jim Reeves, Basil Bacon, Jimmy Houston, Johnny Morris and Gene Taylor. His float business and Devil's Dive Resort which he owned from 1967 to 2001 have been featured in numerous magazine and newspaper articles and on many regional TV and radio fishing shows.

In his 44 years of floating, J.D. says he has been blessed to enjoy so much time on the water fishing with his many friends. In 1969, J.D.'s son Jeff was born. J.D. says when he brought his new baby boy home, he weighed 32 pounds on his fish scale. Jeff Fletcher learned so much from his father, he embarked on a successful professional angling career including a trip to the Bassmasters Classic in 1996. J.D. still manages Devil's Dive Resort on the upper White of Table Rock, guides float trips on the White and Kings, seines minnows and even runs his trot line daily. He is now teaching his two grandsons to fish.

The Ozarks are renown for their float fishing. For a hundred years, people have enjoyed floating and fishing the many fine streams of these hills. Whether to enjoy the beauty of the hills and valleys, watch a smallmouth leap from the water's surface or simply experience the serenity of a fog floating across a river's surface, locals and visitors alike continue to appreciate these fine waters.

Chapter 4
Taming the White

When man first inhabited the White River Valley, he lived near water. Man has always desired to cross the water and has always tried to overcome the relentless flow. The native Americans and earliest white men in this area crossed the White and its tributaries on foot or horseback, usually at the shallowest locations. Early inhabitants also used dugout canoes, rafts or small boats to cross the rivers. Crossings were always done at some risk. The risk increased considerably during floods or high water.

As settlers moved into the White River area, ferries were established at major crossings. Possibly the first major ferry was along the Wilderness Road at the present site of Kimberling City. This ferry existed before the Civil War and operated continuously until the White River bridge was built in 1927. Coombs Ferry at Indian Point operated as a backup and alternate route to the Kimberling crossing. Tibbets Ferry was used near Cow Creek.

Many crossings existed where important routes intersected the rivers or market travel necessitated a ford. Some fords were low water crossings, some had cable ferries and some were paved routes. On the James there were fords just above the White at the Philibert Homestead, Oswalt Ford, Carr Ford at Buttermilk Bay, Stewart Ford, Wilson Ford near Piney Creek, Cole Ford, Hanes Ford, Melton and Miller Ford near Cape Fair and Lower Stone Ford.

On the Kings there was Prentice Ford just downstream from the present 86 bridge, Garrison Ford near Sweetwater and Viola Ford. On the White, Morris Ford at Shell Knob was often operated as a ferry. Smith Ford at Viney Creek, Cotner Ford at Owl Creek and Calloway Ford above Eagle Rock all crossed the White River.

A James River ferry, early 20th century. Note johnboats.

With the advent of automobiles, highway bridges were constructed along major routes over the rivers and creeks. The James was spanned at Cape Fair by a bridge on old Route C. Long Creek had bridges on Route P at Oasis and on Hwy. 86 near Jakes Branch. Big Indian Creek had three low water bridges including one on old Hwy. 86. At one time there was a cable and wood pedestrian bridge spanning Big Indian at McCullough school.

The White River bridge on Hwy. 13 was built in 1927. The Townsend Bridge crossed at Philibert Bluff. The White River bridge at Shell Knob provided access across the river near the mouth of the Kings. Near the present site of Big M, a bridge built in 1929 crossed the White on old Hwy. 39. Farwell Bridge was the crossing at Eagle Rock. The Y-bridge at Cape Fair was constructed in 1927.

All of these fords, ferries and bridges were covered by the waters of Table Rock Reservoir. Although very little evidence of these structures can be seen today, they remain a testament to man's desire to get from one side of the river to the other.

In 1901 the town of Hollister, Missouri surveyed a site on the

Dedication of the Y bridge at Galena 1927

The White River bridge at Shell Knob, 1940's.

upper White River for a hydroelectric dam. The first proposal to dam the White and James Rivers was introduced in Congress in 1906. As early as 1907, private investors considered a dam at the "Table Rock" site upstream from Branson. The name Table Rock referred to a large rock outcrop on Table Rock Mountain above the White River near the present dam site. Today, this formation is the location of a scenic overlook above Lake Taneycomo.

The Ozark Power and Water Company realized this dream when they began construction of Powersite Dam near Forsyth in 1911. The lake formed, Taneycomo, backed up the White for 22 miles. Powersite Dam's gates were first closed on May 9, 1913. Within two days, water was flowing over the top of the dam. This event would portend the way Table Rock filled up.

Shortly after completion of Powersite, the Empire District Electric Company took over control of the dam. Empire District was interested in building a larger hydroelectric project and began buying parcels of bottomland along the upper White. In 1929, The Springfield Mirror reported that Empire District was very close to approval of a Table Rock dam project. The proposed dam was similar to the one ultimately built, damming the White to a pool elevation of 900'. The Mirror reported the purchase of land in the basin by both Empire District and private speculators. The only problem they foresaw delaying the start of the project was a dispute with Stone County over the replacement of roads and bridges. Obviously, the problems were greater.[8] Public opposition, lack of financing and difficulty in finding a suitable dam site deterred their efforts and they lost their permit to build in 1935. During this period, interest increased in taming the White through federal funding.

Heavily logged-over terrain, poor agricultural practices and the draining of swamp lands contributed to periodic damaging floods in the White River valley. In 1941, Congress approved a four-dam flood control and hydroelectric power project on the White.

Norfork was the first constructed in 1944. Bull Shoals was started in 1947 and completed in 1951. Flooding still occurred on the upper White due to the large watershed, heavy rains and the inability of the existing dams to control the large amounts of runoff. Despite the floods, there was always opposition to large dam building. Local people were concerned about the loss of farmland, reduced tax revenues, loss of wildlife habitat and fluctuating water levels.

Several sites were considered for Table Rock Dam. The present site was selected and work began on the dam and lake basin in 1954. Concrete work started in 1955. The dam was completed in 1958. The finished dam has 1602 feet of concrete and 4821 feet of earthen and rock embankment. The gravity dam rises 252 feet above the river bed. The total cost for the project was $65,420,000.

Beaver Lake was impounded in 1964. With the completion of Beaver, all of the White River in Missouri and significant parts in Arkansas were impounded. This section of the White would never flow free again. However, flooding was mostly controlled, cheap electricity was being generated and an exceptional fishing and recreation area was created.

It is worth mentioning that Dewey Short, U.S. Representative from Galena, Missouri fought for many years for the construction of Table Rock Dam. Even when the project was delayed significantly by the Depression and World War II, Short continued to fight for support of the project. To honor his dedication, in 1984 the U.S. House passed a bill naming the visitor's center at Table Rock Dam in honor of Dewey Short.

Completed Table Rock Dam

Chapter 5
Construction and Development of Table Rock

Construction of Table Rock Dam was authorized by the U.S. Congress by the Flood Control Act of 1941 for "flood control and hydroelectric power, and other beneficial water uses". Due to World War II, the Korean War and the Corps' decision to build Bull Shoals first, Table Rock was delayed for 13 years. Construction of the project was done by Morrison-Knudsen Company, Inc. and Utah Construction Company.

Table Rock's lake bed consisted of large forested areas and some river bottomland prior to the dam's construction. The area to be inundated was typical Ozark highland forest with primarily mixed hardwood and cedar trees. The White River bottomland contained many small farms and homesteads. The U.S. government purchased all private land within the project's boundaries.

Land purchases began in the early 50's and were finalized in 1961. 43,000 acres up to the planned conservation pool elevation of 915 feet comprised most of the lake basin. Acreage between 915' and 931', the flood control pool level, required acquisition of 9200 acres. An additional 5,501 acres above 931' comprised flowage easement rights. Flowage easement parcels, which may be periodically flooded by Table Rock, can be privately owned, but not developed. The total project acreage, excluding easements, was 57,806.

The purchase of private land caused considerable consternation among many inhabitants of the White River valley. Many families had lived on family farms for generations. Many would lose their homes. Some residents welcomed the opportunity to sell.

In 1955, the Corps opened a real estate office in Branson to acquire project land. They also published a booklet and held public meetings explaining their purchase policies. Nevertheless, there was much confusion on the issues. There was particular misunderstanding about the obtaining of property between 923 and 936 feet elevations. These acquisitions involved a complicated formula involving flowage easements, topography and land contour changes.

The Corps contacted all land owners with an offer for their property. Some accepted, some refused. When the owners refused, the property was condemned and seized.

Bob Philibert of Shell Knob grew corn and ran some stock on a farm near the present site of Pla-Port resort. He was offered $20 an acre for the land by the U.S. government in the early 50's. Bob felt this was an unfair price and refused it. Under these circumstances, the government was forced to condemn the land and take ownership under eminent domain. This procedure required that three appraisals be made on the property and the owner paid the highest price. Mr. Philibert followed this route as apparently many other landowners did to receive the best price for their land.

Land owners were allowed to remain on their property until the project required them to leave. Those who accepted the government's offer could stay for a specified period. Those who forced condemnation proceedings could remain on the land under a lease. Most were allowed to stay on the property until October 1956. Some who refused to sell were ordered off by April 1956. This apparent discrimination was opposed and ultimately the Corps changed this policy.

About 4600 acres of Mark Twain National Forest were transferred to the Corps of Engineers. 3294 acres of this land was a large tract in the Cow Creek area. The remaining acreage ceded consisted of many small parcels within the lake's boundaries up to the 936 feet flowage easement. In 1954, there were four small settlements, several schools and cemeteries, numerous homes and farm buildings, miles of roads and several bridges in the flood zone of Table Rock Lake.

Between 1951 and 1955, the University of Missouri and the Missouri Archaeological Society made several surveys of the project lands. The first major dig to salvage cultural antiquities was at Rice Shelter in 1952. Many others were soon initiated. Grants from the National Park Service and a Congressional allocation of $25,000 in 1955 helped support considerable archaeological activity. In 1957, the University of Arkansas Museum in Fayetteville began digs on sites in Arkansas that would be inundated by Table Rock. These efforts continued even after the dam was started. Known as the Table Rock Salvage Project, thousands of artifacts were saved, helping preserve the cultural remnants of the native and pioneer dwellers of the White River valley.

Only about 5% of the standing timber in the lake bed was cleared. There were two opposing public views on the amount of forest to be removed. People who looked forward to using the lake for boating, skiing, scuba diving and swimming favored removal of all timber. Fishermen and wildlife proponents preferred leaving as many trees as possible. The Corps eventually decided on a policy to remove trees that would remain above water in the main channels. This was primarily on land between elevation 874' and 915'. By following this approach, most of the main lake areas required minimal basin clearing due to the water's depth. Clearing was done down to elevation 840' around planned recreation areas. In many coves and feeder streams, the timber was left in place. Of course, many areas along the rivers had already been cleared for agriculture. In fact, photographs of some areas prior to the lake show considerably more cleared land than they do today. The forested areas left in Table Rock's lake basin were estimated at 11,000 acres.

Most work performed in the lake bed was done by contract under supervision of the Corps of Engineers. Some bridges were removed by the state or county. Some buildings and structures were removed or demolished by their owners, others by contracted construction firms and many were never removed. The flood of 1957 found many structures remaining in the project boundaries. Many of these buildings were destroyed by the rising water- one of these, the old grist mill at Oasis. The Two Rivers Camp near Shell Knob owned by V.L. Erard was destroyed. One of the camp cabins was seen floating away. Crops still being raised in the bottomlands were destroyed. When the water was lowered, most of the remaining trees in the lake basin had been killed. Everything left standing was coated with mud. Reports from this time indicate fishing was already good in the premature lake. People also reported lots of wildlife, including snakes, fleeing the rising water.

One of the most sensitive issues necessitated by the building of Table Rock Lake was the relocation of cemeteries. This work involving disinterment, moving and reinterment of remains was contracted, but closely supervised by the Corps. 1132 graves from 49 burial sites were moved. Many of these sites were small with as few as one grave. The largest cemetery relocated contained the remains of 134. Relocation was to eight new or enlarged cemeteries. Monuments, fences and markers were also moved.

The Table Rock project included plans for 23 public use areas: Aunts Creek, Baxter, Beaver, Big Indian, Big M, Campbell Point, Cape Fair, Coombs Ferry, Cow Creek, Cricket Creek, Eagle Rock, Hwy 13, Indian Point, James River, Joe Bald, Kings River, Long Creek, Mill Creek, Old 86, Owens, Viney Creek, Viola and Table Rock State Park. James River and Owens were never opened. Big Bay was developed by the U.S. Forest Service in 1964. The Corps of Engineers contracted the recreational areas to be partially cleared, boat ramps and roads constructed and some restrooms and water facilities built. After completion of the dam, Corps Operation and Maintenance improved the campsites.

Marina concessions were offered at eleven sites. It was originally hoped that nearby towns would "adopt" these marinas and develop and promote the facilities. Early maps of the lake often show these town names associated with the marinas. The concessions were to be awarded by bidding. The successful bidders constructed and developed the marinas and paid a percentage of the gross revenues to the Corps. The cities were never successful in bidding or operating the facilities and soon all were owned by private individuals. All the original commercial marinas are still operating successfully.

Over the years, several of the recreational areas on Table Rock have been closed. Due to budgetary restraints, some of the less popular sites were shut down. Big Indian, Coombs Ferry and Kings River are no longer operated for public use. The boat ramps at these locations are still used frequently. Beaver campground has been operated under lease by the town of Beaver for 25 years. Cow Creek was closed to the general public, but is leased for group camping.

Originally, there was no limit on the size or location of private docks on Table Rock. Dock permits have always been required. In 1972, the Corps developed the first Shoreline Management Plan. It restricted private docks to about 10% of the shoreline, primarily in coves and near developments. This plan is reviewed every five years and modified as needed. Presently, the amount of Table Rock's shoreline available for private boat docks is about 11-12%. In 1982, the minimum size of a dock was set at 12 slips. Since then, additional regulations have been enacted including sealed flotation, grounded electrical supply, orientation, land access and parking. The value of dock permits and boat slips has increased steadily on the lake as demand rose and availability decreased.

Many caves, mines, sinkholes and springs were covered by Table Rock's waters. The following letter written by Cloy Brazle to the Shell Knob Rattler newspaper in 1981 describes one cave near Shell Knob. Although not inundated, this cave is typical of some of the stories told in these hills. Mr. Brazle was 79 years old when he wrote this account (original spelling):

"I grew up to manhood south of Shell Knob and some cousins and I found a cave near the Turkey Mountain Estates. There was some skelitens, several army rifles inside.

We could not tell about it for we were not supposed to be off the farm. I have talked to a man that lived across the river that watched through a telescope seen men go in and out of this cave he lived in western Kansas.

After the lake was formed I took a professor up the lake in a boat found the cave but the mouth of the cave was filled with a pack rats nest. So we got another boat the next day at the steel bridge at mouth of mill creek took a garden scratcher to dig out the nest but when I started I raked out three snakes (snakes is a birth mark to me) the shelf is less than three feet wide and over a hundred feet down So I quit and I think that I was the last person to be inside that cave and I feel that those skelitons and guns have been hid long enough. The three cousins that were with me are deceased now.

It was 1914 when I was in the cave last. I have read of the cave in two books one called it a robers hide out and the other book called it a confedart army hide out and Indians may have used it before that.

The cave mouth is the size of a large wash tub the room inside is some 30 ft has a spring inside for their water."

There are numerous legends around Table Rock about buried treasure and lost mines. Some of these troves traced back to the Native Americans, while others were of more recent vintage. A silver mine was reported near Eagle Rock on what would become the Farwell property. The location is now reportedly under water. Another legend involved Indians and Spanish explorers mining silver at a location on Bread Tray Mountain near present day Baxter. If the tale is true, this site could still be on dry land. One story is told of a thief burying stolen gold coins near the Kimberling ferry.

Perhaps the most famous tale is of the Yocum silver dollars. There is no doubt the Yocums produced silver coins. The exact location of their source for the metal has been sought by many fortune hunters. The mine is generally placed somewhere between Reeds Spring and Joe Bald.

The Ozarks has many tales and legends. When a project the size of Table Rock is built, many historical sites are flooded. It is perhaps this concealment that spawns the interest in buried treasure.

Table Rock dam is a combination concrete-gravity and earth/rock embankment structure. The concrete portion begins on the south side of the valley against the high rock bluffs and spans 1602 feet. The remaining portion of the barrier is 4821 feet of rock and dirt fill. The concrete section consists of huge concrete monoliths poured in place on bedrock, considerably wider at the bottom than at the top. The dam consists of 1,230,000 cubic yards of concrete and 3,320,000 cubic yards of embankment. The top of the dam is at elevation 947' above sea level. At normal pool of 915', the water is 220 feet deep at the face of the dam. Table Rock is considered a deep, highland type reservoir. The main channel is over 100' deep in many locations. At the Hwy. 13 bridge, the water is about 185 feet deep. The depth at Shell Knob is around 105'. The water reaches about 75 feet at both the Cape Fair and Eagle Rock bridges. Normal water flow is through four 50,000 kilowatt generating units. The penstock openings are about 140 feet below the surface of Table Rock Lake. The dam also has ten floodgates which allow the release of large amounts of water during flood conditions.

Work on the dam began in 1954. The dam site was excavated across the White River valley floor. In addition to several construction buildings, a refrigeration and concrete mixing plant were erected on the south bluff. Cable-way towers were constructed on both sides of the valley.

On the north end of the dam, the rock and dirt embankment was raised by trucking in thousands of loads of fill. On the south end, a five foot notch was blasted into the bluff wall to act as an anchor for the dam. By the spring of 1955, there were about 700 men working at the dam site. Many local men were employed on the project. Concrete pouring began in May.

Table Rock Dam was poured in sections called monoliths. Aggregate rock was quarried from Baird Mountain and crushed into 6, 3, 1, ¾, ½, ¼ inch and sand sizes. This aggregate was transported to the dam site by a huge conveyor belt system. All of the crushed rock except sand was run through tanks and cooled with 37 degree F. water. It was then transferred to insulated bins at the mixing plant. Rock, sand, cement and flake ice were combined in 4 cubic yard mixers. The use of cooling water and ice was necessary to control the temperature of the concrete. If the concrete was poured at too high a temperature, cracking would have occurred, weakening the structure.

After mixing, the concrete was placed in 8 cubic yard buckets sitting on a railroad car and moved to the traveling cable-way tower on the south side. This cable system had a 25 ton capacity. The buckets were attached to the cable and moved to the proper location above the dam by the operator. When positioned properly, the concrete was poured into the monolith forms. Most of the concrete is not reinforced except around openings.

Every effort was made to keep the concrete pouring almost continuously. At one point, a windstorm blew the traveling tower off its track and delayed pouring for several days. By the summer of 1955 there were about 950 men working on the dam.

In addition to the work on the dam, the power plant and switch-yard were constructed simultaneously on the north, downstream side. On the Taneycomo side of the structure, a stilling basin was created. The river bed and walls below the dam were reinforced with concrete to avoid erosion. Several concrete baffle blocks were placed in the stilling basin to break up the flow of water passing through the dam. Water passing through the four conduits at the base of the dam flows at 90 mph when the conduit gates are wide open. Water can also flow through the generator penstocks and the spillway/floodgate combination.

In June of 1957, the incomplete dam was topped by flood waters. The mighty structure held and construction was completed in 1958. The hydroelectric plant was completed and on-line in 1959. The project was dedicated in 1959.[9]

The Table Rock Project had been a dream of area residents, local politicians, speculators and sportsmen for decades. When finally completed, it was a shining example of what could be accomplished by man when working with nature. Table Rock Lake was destined to become one of the best fishing lakes in the country and one of the most popular vacation destinations. Flooding in the White River had finally been controlled. Hydroelectric power was being generated for a growing area. Table Rock Lake would become the driving force behind the economic boom developing in this area of the Ozarks.

The water flowing through Table Rock Dam's penstocks and out through the draft tubes enters Taneycomo at a temperature of about 45 degrees F. year-round. This situation forever changed the nature of Lake Taneycomo.

Taneycomo had been an excellent warm water fishery since Powersite Dam began backing up the White in 1913. Known pri-

Blasting the notch for the dam on the south bluff

Dam under construction. Note the monoliths in various stages including the penstocks, the cable-way tower, the cement plant and the concrete bucket.

The lake overflowing the incomplete dam in 1957.
Note construction of the generator section.

View below the dam. Note the baffle blocks and penstock conduits.

View of the downstream side of Table Rock Dam. Note the embankment structure and powerplant under construction.

View of the spillway with one gate wide open. Compare to size of people on dam roadway.

Downstream side of dam January, 1958.

Project dedication ceremony 1959. Note photos of President Eisenhower, Senator Symington and Representative Short.

marily for its bass and crappie fishing, Taneycomo had attracted anglers for many years. Float fishermen had been plying the White for decades. Branson was often the take-out point for floats on the upper White. Sometimes, floaters would continue fishing on Taneycomo, portage around Powersite Dam and continue their trip down the river.

Table Rock modified Taneycomo in many ways. The cold water made the small lake mostly unsuitable for bass and other warm water fishes. To remedy this, Taneycomo was converted into a trout lake. To maintain the fishery, Shepherd of the Hills Trout Hatchery was developed on 211 acres just below Table Rock Dam. Rainbow and brown trout reared in the hatchery are stocked regularly into Taneycomo to maintain the population. This fishery has earned a reputation as one of the most popular trout lakes in the country.

The dam influenced Taneycomo in other ways. Water flow is affected by the amount of releases from Table Rock. These releases, based on electricity needs and lake levels create variable current conditions on Taneycomo. Due to the constraints of the little lake's size and development along the lake, its level rarely varies more than plus or minus five feet. The Table Rock releases also affect oxygen concentrations in Taneycomo. These factors are important to the fishery and cause considerable interest in those concerned about the little lake's life.

In addition to Hwy. 165 which crosses over the dam, Table Rock is spanned by five major bridges: the Long Creek Bridge on Hwy. 86, the Hwy. 13 bridge at Kimberling City, the Central Crossing Bridge at Shell Knob, the Hwy. 76 bridge at Cape Fair and the Hwy. 86 bridge at Eagle Rock.

There are also several smaller bridges crossing the tributaries impounded by Table Rock Lake. In Arkansas, there is a concrete bridge over Yocum Creek on County Road 311 and at Beaver, the interesting one-lane steel and wood suspension bridge. This old bridge sometimes called the "Golden Gate Bridge" was erected in 1949. There are two smaller spans on Hwy. 173 north of Cape Fair. Highway 86 crosses the Kings River east of Carr Lane and Roaring River just north of Eagle Rock.

There are many interesting stories about the building of these bridges and the old bridges, ferries and fords they replaced. Present day maps indicate the sites of at least 16 fords, two ferries and 11 bridges were flooded when the lake was filled. Undoubtably, there were many more historic crossings that existed long before the reservoir was built.

Although not technically over Table Rock, the Y-bridge at Galena has an interesting history. This concrete span built in 1927 replaced two previous bridges over the James. Dewey Short spoke at the dedication ceremony. The bridge still exists and is on the National Register of Historic Places. Today, traffic crosses the river at Galena on a concrete structure erected in 1986.

The longest bridge over Table Rock, the Kimberling City bridge, replaced the White River bridge built in 1927 on Hwy.13 at Radical. Prior to 1927, John Kimberling operated a ferry at the same site. This point on the White has been a crossing location at least since the Wilderness Road which existed prior to the Civil War. Table Rock filled so fast prematurely in 1957 that for a few months, the new bridge was not finished and the old bridge was under water. During this period, army personnel from Ft. Wood operated a ferry at the site. The old bridge, although sold for scrap, was never removed and is still under the water at Kimberling.

The Central Crossing Bridge at Shell Knob was not in the original plans for lake development. Pleas from Shell Knob and Viola citizens and the support of Senator Stuart Symington and Congressman Dewey Short convinced the Corps of Engineers to add the bridge late in the project process. Construction began in 1957. As at Hwy.13, there was a period when the new bridge was incomplete and the old bridge was inundated. Eventually, the lake level was brought down enough to allow the old White River bridge (built in 1927 on then Hwy. 86) to be dynamited out. During the time that both bridges were unuseable, local residents had to drive several miles around the lake to travel between Shell Knob and Viola. One source indicated that a Shell Knob School teacher traveled to school each day by means of the equipment ferry used to construct the new bridge. Others were ferried across by motorboat. A ferry was requested at this site, but the Corps decided the access was too difficult.

The old Shell Knob bridge under water 1957

The first bridge over Long Creek was constructed by Taney County prior to 1920, but was unused for several years. Some time after 1922, acceptable road access to this bridge was developed and the one-lane span was opened for use. For years prior to Table Rock Lake, the settlement of Oasis (previously Cedar Valley) existed near the site of this bridge. There were two fords, Deep Ford and Shallow Ford, near the Oasis mill site at Goat Hill. The bridge at this location eventually became the Route P crossing over Long Creek. When the lake came, Oasis was drowned. All that can be seen today is the top of Goat Hill, a small island about one mile north of the new Long Creek Bridge. Old Hwy.86 crossed Long Creek near Jakes Branch. The old highway 86 roadbed now provides a boat launching ramp on the north side of the lake.

The old Farwell bridge at Eagle Rock was demolished in place. Approaches to the old bridge can still be seen below the new Hwy.

86 crossing. The span crossing the James at Cape Fair on Route C was removed and replaced with the new bridge on the rerouted Hwy. 76.

The bridge on old 39 near Mano was still in place during the high water conditions of 1957. Rube Dick operated a ferry at this site while the bridge was unuseable. Shortly afterward, the structure was demolished in-place, leaving the rubble on the lake bed.

The new bridges over Table Rock Lake were primarily built by construction firms under contract to the state. The Central Crossing Bridge at Shell Knob was one of the last constructed. This span was built by Rolla Construction of St. Louis starting in 1957, under the inspection of the State of Missouri.

Duke Sherfy an employee of Rolla Construction worked as an equipment operator and labor foreman on this project. Duke described the following construction sequence. After surveying an acceptable crossing, the White River was diverted by temporary weir dams. At the location for each pier, forms were constructed and footings were excavated up to 78 feet into the river bedrock. Most of this work was performed by hand operated air jacks while pumps removed the water from the pits. Concrete was poured to form the footings.

The piers were formed of highly reinforced concrete poured in sections. Moveable forms were used to allow a nearly continuous pour of a gravel, sand, cement and water mix. All gravel and sand was trucked to the site from a Berryville quarry. The concrete was mixed at a concrete plant constructed at the bridge site. Concrete was moved to the pouring location on a cable-way system. A large tower was built on each side of the river, perfectly aligned with the bridge span. A bucket skiff suspended from the cable-way traveled between the towers. The skiff, used to transport men, concrete, steel and other materials, was operated by the "bellboy" in the skiff and the cable-way operator on shore. These two men communicated by walkie- talkie.

Each pier was poured to a certain height and then "capped" with a block. The next slightly smaller section was then poured on top of the cap. Steel "rockers" were attached to the top of the main piers and "sliders" on the two smaller end piers. These members provided

The Central Crossing Bridge under construction.

support and allowed movement of the bridge superstructure. The bridge was built from pre-fabricated steel beams bolted and hot riveted in place. All steel was sandblasted and painted.

The roadbed was poured in place on hanging forms. The bridge floor was asphalted and road approaches completed. Missouri constructed a re-routed Highway 39 across the bridge.

Projects like the Central Crossing Bridge provided employment for many local men. Those hired to work on this bridge joined the union and were paid $1.90 an hour. Although a good wage at the time, this was very difficult and dangerous work. Duke Sherfy relates a story of a terrible fire that occurred during the building of Shell Knob's new bridge.

While pouring pier #3, five men including Duke were inside the forms on Christmas Day repairing the protective tarps. It was necessary to keep the fresh concrete warm using the tarps and propane heaters to assure proper curing. A fire occurred burning all five men seriously. One later died as a result of his injuries. Duke reported one other man died during bridge construction from a fall.

It should be remembered that the beautiful lake, dam, bridges and roads of Table Rock that we enjoy today were the result of the blood, sweat and tears of many hard-working people. Some even gave their lives on this project.

Table Rock has a reputation for clear, clean water. The water quality is determined almost entirely by the nature of the watershed. Table Rock Lake drains over 4000 square miles of the Ozarks. Much of this land is heavily forested and undeveloped. This type of topography generally produces clear run-off and results in clear lake water. Many of the small streams draining into the lake are spring-fed, further contributing to clear conditions.

Agriculture in the watershed tends to reduce water clarity by two means. First, run-off from cultivated lands contributes silt-laden water through erosion. Secondly, fertilized farm and pasture land supply nutrients to the water flowing into the reservoir. Nutrients make the lake more productive and darker.

The Ozark Highlands which comprise most of Table Rock's watershed are of the karst type topography. Karst is characterized by thin soils, porous rock layers, caves and sinkholes. Water moves quickly through these formations. Polluted or silt-laden water has less chance to be filtered before entering the lake. This makes Table Rock more sensitive to contaminates from the watershed..

Human development around the lake has had a negative influence on water clarity. As early as the 1930's, Sullivan[10] reported pollution in the James River from Springfield sewage. As the Table Rock Lake area has developed over the years, the levels of pollution and nutrients from sewage treatment plants, septic systems, agricultural and livestock production, construction, highway development and other point and non-point sources have increased.

Even though Table Rock is considered to have and deserves its reputation for clean water, some areas of the lake have never had clear water. The James and Kings arms have always contained darker water due to their nutrient loads. These two arms are also considered the most productive fisheries. Clear water does not really make for the best fishing. Clean water is important of course, but a more productive area will generally be the best for fishing. Prior to Beaver Dam, the upper White portion of Table Rock was darker and more like the Kings. After Beaver, this area ran clear more often and the fishery changed somewhat.

Water clarity and cleanliness also affect the predominance of different fish species. Largemouth bass prefer darker water. Kentucky bass will inhabit various habitats, but seem to prefer clearer water. Smallmouth are definitely partial to clear conditions. Walleye usually have a predilection for water that is less colored. Fishermen usually prefer some color to the water. Very clear conditions can make fish spooky and fishing more difficult. Muddy conditions can make it harder for fish to see or find a bait and therefore make fishing tougher.

Perhaps the beauty of Table Rock is that it has a variety of water conditions. Anglers have several options to choose from throughout the lake ranging from shallow to deep, clear to cloudy and heavy cover to clean banks.

Chapter 6
The 1960's

When the quickly rising water began filling Table Rock's lake bed prematurely in 1957, unbelievable amounts of underwater cover were created. Only about 5% of the original standing timber in the lake basin had been cleared.

Much of this cleared timber was bulldozed into huge piles and burned. Many areas of the lake bed had been previously cleared bottomland, but large tracts of timbered land remained, particularly along the creeks and steep bluffs. In addition to trees and smaller vegetation, the lake covered the remains of hundreds of buildings and fences, scores of old roadbeds and numerous bridges. Most structures were demolished and burned during construction, but foundations and rubble were left in many locations. This abundant cover created perfect habitat for gamefish.

Other than the release of 8 million walleye fry, there were no initial stocking programs during development or the early existence of Table Rock. The fish populations developed from the existing fisheries in the rivers and streams. The indigenous fish in Table Rock were rainbow trout, walleye, pickerel, carp, buffalo, suckers, channel, blue, bullhead and flathead catfish, green and longear sunfish, bluegill, drum, gar, black and white crappie, white bass and rock, spotted, smallmouth and largemouth bass. For the most part, these populations developed well in the wide variety of habitats and extensive cover in the newly formed lake. Huge areas of flooded brush provided excellent spawning sites for the first few years. Along with the many stream minnows and darters, gizzard shad helped make up a baitfish population. Threadfin shad were established in Table Rock from existing populations in Lake Springfield, Long Creek and later, Beaver Lake.

The lake level rose to 896 feet above sea level in June of 1957 due to heavy rains. There was concern about the effect this huge amount of water would have on the as yet uncompleted dam. Water actually ran over the top of the structure. There was a large V-shaped notch in the center of the dam that had not been poured yet. Fortunately, the monolithic dam was not damaged.

By October of that year, the lake was de-watered back down to 726 feet to complete work on the dam, bridges and accesses. The level rose again to 816' in April 1958 and lowered again. By the end of 1958, Table Rock was filling permanently. It first reached normal pool of 915' in May 1960. Once filled, Table Rock reached its historic high and low level in the 60's. In May of 1961, the water peaked at 932.49 feet. In February 1965, the lowest level of 881.54 feet was reached.

Lake levels varied considerably during the 1960's providing a variety of conditions and challenges for anglers. Table Rock is a large reservoir and in the early years still contained large amounts of visible standing timber. Most boats of this era were small with limited horsepower. The lake was huge, but most anglers didn't have to go very far to find good fishing spots.

Ralph Lambert developed Kings Harbor Resort on the Kings River along with his wife Mary and her parents in 1959. In the spring of 1960, the lake level was about 900' or 15 feet below normal pool. Ralph didn't own his own tackle at the time, but liked to borrow his wife's gear which included a Pfleuger Supreme reel. He fished from the shore using a River Runt plug and caught lots of fish. He remembers catching crappie, white bass and black bass up to three pounds.

In the first few years of Table Rock, fish were increasing in number and size. By 1961, the lake level had risen to several feet above normal pool. Numerous resorts were operating on the lake. In 1960, there were an estimated 125 new motels and 2000 homes around the lake. In 1964, Table Rock had about 3 million visitors. By 1965, there were 150 motels/resorts operating. Table Rock was quickly developing a reputation for great fishing- particularly for bass and crappie.

Colvin reported that an excellent crappie fishery developed in the James River area of Table Rock in the early years. Harvests during the 1960's often exceeded 25 fish per acre. The highest harvest rate of 84 fish per acre occurred in 1964. The James arm quickly gained a reputation for producing large harvests and large-sized crappie.[11] There was no length limit on crappie at this time and the daily limit was 30. Large numbers of crappie were taken from Table Rock. Hanson reported that in 1960, 44% of the total fish taken from Long Creek were crappie. In 1964, crappie made up 73% of the total creel from the James River Arm.[12] Obviously, lots of anglers were fishing for and catching crappie on Table Rock.

This degree of harvesting and the variability in spawning success from year to year eventually led to a dramatic decrease in the crappie population. Later on, attempts would be made to improve crappie fishing through length and possession limits.

Hanson[13] reported on an extensive creel survey done on Table Rock Reservoir from 1959 through 1969. This report gives a very good picture of the amount of fishing, success rates, types of fish caught, methods, water conditions and source of anglers. Hanson's study covered the lake effectively through surveys done at Long Creek, Indian Point, the James River and the upper White between Eagle Rock and Big M. This comprehensive work gives an excellent account of what fishing was like on Table Rock during the decade of the 60's.

Creel surveys were performed in Long Creek starting in 1959. Fishing was very heavy in this area the first three years and then began to decrease with slight increases in 1966 and 1969. The total catch of fish followed a similar pattern. Crappie, bluegill and black bass accounted for most of the fish caught. Crappie were by far the most numerous. Largemouth bass were much more common than either spotted or smallmouth. Catfish accounted for only a small portion of the creel.[14] It's possible that catfish were undercounted in this survey. Catfish were often taken at night and on trot lines used at hours not covered by the creel survey.

The Indian Point area had results very similar to Long Creek. This area was surveyed starting in 1961, a very heavily fished year

51

with large numbers of fish taken. The water in this area was very deep and clear with Secchi disk readings of 15 feet common.

Hanson's report on the James River creel survey covered an area around Cape Fair. The James River contained more productive, nutrient-laden water than the other areas in the survey. This factor and its somewhat more isolated location influenced its development and success as a fishery. Fishing trips to the James started somewhat later, but developed quickly. The James maintained its position as a desirable angling destination throughout most of the 60's. The types of fish caught, primarily crappie, bluegill and bass, maintained their numbers better during the decade.[15]

The upper White region had less fishing pressure and poorer results. Before Beaver Dam was completed , the upper White was fairly colored. After 1964, the water was clearer and colder. This appeared to have a negative impact, at least on the fishermen, as the number of fishing trips and fish caught dropped dramatically in 1965. These numbers improved somewhat toward the end of the decade.[16]

The building of Beaver Dam also created a new fishery on the very upper end of the White River on Table Rock. As with Table Rock Dam, Beaver's tailrace made an excellent trout fishery with its clear, cold water. Regular stocking of trout by the Arkansas Fish & Game Commission maintains the population.

The types of fish caught in Table Rock during the early years are well reflected in the creel surveys. As previously noted, crappie were by far the most common fish taken. Large numbers of bluegill and sunfish were a significant part of the creel. Largemouth were easily the black bass most commonly possessed. Lakewide, they accounted for at least 80% of this species caught. Spotted or Kentucky bass made up about 20% of the black bass creel in the 60's. Surprisingly, smallmouth were rarely caught anywhere in Table Rock.

White bass were taken by anglers in fairly good numbers early in this period, but their numbers dropped throughout the decade. Channel and flathead catfish were not caught in any great amount until 1968. This may reflect an increase in the use of trot and jug lines as an angling technique.

Despite early attempts to introduce walleye into Table Rock, few were ever taken. A few rainbow trout were taken during this survey. Most of these probably came from three sources: release of excess fingerlings from the Shepherd of the Hills hatchery into Table Rock in 1966 and 1967, fish migrating out of Roaring River and trout introductions into the upper White below Beaver by Arkansas.

The number of anglers fishing with natural or live bait was greater than those using artificials during the 1960's. This difference was particularly noticeable early on, but began to change throughout this period and by 1968 the ratio reversed. The number of live bait anglers remained higher in the James River than other locations. This may have been due to the popularity of crappie fishing and the source of anglers in this area. Trolling, primarily for white bass, was used fairly consistently during the 60's. Set lines were almost unheard of in this report until 1968. Most anglers fished from boats, but some did fish from the shore. The ratio of boat to shore fishermen stayed about 10 to 1 during the first decade of Table Rock.

One final part of Hanson's study looked at the origin of anglers fishing the reservoir. Fishermen came from local areas, Missouri's metropolitan areas, throughout the state and out-of-state. Some even came from other nations. Metropolitan visitors tended to congregate in the Indian Point and James River areas. Long Creek and the upper White had greater numbers of local anglers. Out-of-state fishermen tended to visit areas throughout the lake.

Hanson concludes his comprehensive report on creel surveys by stating that a length limit of about 12 inches on largemouth bass should be considered. His foresight was partially predicated on the expected increase in fishing pressure and angling skill in the years to come on Table Rock.

Walleye existed in the watershed of Table Rock prior to impoundment. Over the years, a stocking program has attempted to improve the walleye fishing. Eight million walleye fry were stocked as the lake was being developed. Most of these were lost during the de-watering in 1957 or to predation.

Prior to the lake and in the early sixties, walleye accounted for a small part of the fish caught. Despite early attempts to introduce walleye into Table Rock, this fishery did not develop successfully in most areas of the lake. One exception was the Campbell Point area. In the mid-60's, walleye fishing was reported as very good in this area. Campbell Point Dock reported 62 walleye brought in over a one month period weighing from 4 to 10 pounds each. At one point, Campbell Point promoted this area as the "best walleye fishing in the Ozarks". Whether these fish were from stocking or indigenous walleye is unclear. Whether due to lack of angler effort or reduced population, the number of walleye taken tapered off during the first decade of the lake. By 1970, walleye were almost unheard of at Table Rock. In a report by Hanson[17] on creel surveys done from 1970 to 1972, no walleye were reported from the James River and only 13 were documented from Long Creek. This fishery would remain untapped for several years. Recently, walleye interest has increased as greater numbers and larger fish have been caught.

White bass fishing was good in the early years of the lake. Populations adapted well to the deep, clear waters of Table Rock. Heavy catches of white bass were common, particularly during the spring and fall runs. The Kings, James and Long Creek tributaries have always been the prime locations for white bass. The introduction of threadfin shad into the lake[1] seems to have had a positive impact on white bass angling.

J.D. Fletcher reports that one of his most successful fishing days ever came on the Kings River in 1960. Fishing with a white ⅛ oz. Tiny Tot jig, he caught 50 white bass on 50 casts. A feat like this would be difficult to duplicate, but the kind of white bass schools seen to this day indicate it would be possible to come close.

Because of its generally very clear water and populations of non-game fish, Table Rock was popular for scuba diving and spearfishing. Large fish like carp, gar, buffalo, drum and sucker were taken by underwater methods. In 1969, <u>Skin Diver Magazine</u> reported excellent conditions on Table Rock for spearfishing.

[1]Threadfin shad were introduced into Table Rock form existing lake populations in Lake Springfield, Long Creek and Beaver Lake.

Although clear water is usually preferred for scuba, spearing fish was most successful in dingier areas where fish could be approached stealthily. This article reported a method used to take big carp. Skin divers would choose an area with good water color and standing timber. They would approach near the bottom and then "climb" a tree to spear unwary carp near the surface.

Different areas of the lake achieved different angling results. Prior to Beaver Dam's completion in 1964, the upper White portion of Table Rock had considerably darker water. After Beaver went in, the water became much clearer and colder. The James and Kings Rivers were more productive, eutrophic arms. Despite concerns about water pollution in these areas, the larger load of nutrients made the James and Kings productive fisheries. Long Creek was a fairly clear tributary and being closer to the dam filled more quickly in the early years.

Accessibility was a factor in fishing pressure during the first years of Table Rock. Areas closer to larger towns or more developed tourist areas received greater pressure.

Table Rock Lake has always had a well deserved reputation as a clear, clean lake. Despite this, concerns about water quality can be traced back at least to the 1930's (see page 11, Sullivan study). In the 1960's, William Dieffenbach and Frank Ryck, Jr. performed a water quality survey in the James River basin.[18] Based on their report, Dieffenbach and Ryck used a much more developed scientific approach and reported much more data than did Sullivan. Their findings indicated a much changed waterway in the 30 years since Sullivan's study.

In this study, 19 streams in the Elk, James and Spring River basins were evaluated at 52 sampling stations in 1964. At each station, samples were taken of the bottom-dwelling invertebrates. The density, diversity and composition of these invertebrate communities were used as a gauge of water quality.

Seven streams were sampled in the James River basin. Of these, five were found to have serious pollution problems. Wilson Creek was grossly polluted by the Springfield Southwest Sewage Treatment Plant for five miles. This point-source also was found to seriously affect the water quality of about 15 miles of the upper

James. Two miles of Sequiota Creek were polluted by septic tank and lagoon discharges. Finley Creek had adversely affected water quality for seven miles of its course from sewage and industrial effluent from Ozark. Two miles of Flat Creek were found to be tainted by Cassville sewage lagoon discharges.

Dieffenbach and Ryck did find the conditions improved on the James further downstream. Here they reported heavy algae growths and very high nitrate concentrations. Just below Cassville, their study found high nitrate and phosphate levels, high fecal *coliform* bacteria counts and a noticeable phytoplankton bloom.

This report indicates that there were water quality concerns in the Table Rock watershed very early in the lake's existence. Concerted efforts to improve water quality would not noticeably gain extensive support until many years later. However, the Missouri Department of Conservation certainly had an interest in Table Rock and completed several studies on the fishery.

Bass fishing developed steadily throughout the 60's. Fishing for bass alone did not have the following it does today. Equipment was rudimentary compared to the high-tech tackle available now. Many anglers used open-faced baitcasting reels with braided line on steel or plastic rods. Live bait was used more often than artificials. Those who did use artificial lures cast plugs like the Lucky 13, Crippled Killer, Midge-Oreno, Bass-Oreno, Creek Chub Darter and Dingbat with baitcast reels and caught bass effectively.

During the 60's, more anglers began using closed -faced spinning reels like the Zebco 66 and Johnson #80 with monfilament line on fiberglass rods. This lighter tackle made it possible to cast a wider variety of baits and smaller baits. The introduction of the plastic worm had a huge influence on bass fishing on Table Rock. Early models were often pre-rigged with one to three hooks attached and often a spinner. These baits could be cast easily on the spincast outfits and were deadly on black bass.

The introduction of the Rapala Minnow also had a large impact on Table Rock bassing. Developed in 1960, this lure became wildly popular during the 60's and would eventually lead to the widespread use of similar baits. In part due to the success of the Rapala,

Smithwick and Rebel produced similar "stickbaits" in the mid-60's. Ralph Lambert of Shell Knob relates his early experiences with these lures. He had observed bedding bass in the clear waters of Table Rock, but was having difficulty getting them to take baits like plastic worms, crankbaits or topwaters. He developed an idea to modify a lure to make it suspend and stay in the strike zone longer. Ralph experimented with pinching splitshot onto the hook shanks of a two-hook Rebel. He also tried wrapping solder wire around a Rogue's treble hooks. Ralph found these altered baits to be very effective on pre-spawn and spawning bass. He also experimented with changing the colors on available models with a magic marker. Some of his creations were so successful that he sold them to anglers from his tackle shop at Kings Harbor Resort.

Other baits that saw early development and use on Table Rock were the jig-and-pig, Bomber and Hellbender crankbaits, early spinnerbaits, topwater lures and spoons. These lures were some of the precursors to the highly developed arsenal available to bass anglers today.

If you looked through a hip-roofed metal tackle box of this era, you might find some interesting things. A box of matches or a Zippo lighter were common. A spark plug on a heavy cord made an effective lure retriever. There'd probably be a small tape measure or spring scale, several snelled hooks, plastic or wooden bobbers, a variety of slip sinkers and splitshot, a fillet knife and at least one bottle opener. Chances are a fisherman carried an extra reel and spools of line in his tackle box. If he was over forty, you might find an extra pair of glasses.

In addition to their tackle, most anglers carried some basic equipment. The depth finder was just beginning to be recognized as a useful tool. The aerators available were used for bait containers. Basic aids like nets and homemade plug knockers were common. There was really no specially designed fishing clothing. Anglers wore whatever they had that was suitable for the weather. A smart fisherman at least carried a poncho along for rainy weather. Night fishing was fairly popular. Battery powered spot lights were used for night fishing. Directed over the side of the boat, lights were effective for attracting baitfish and therefore gamefish. Good numbers of crappie and some large bass were taken after hours.

Denver Dixon, present owner of Big M Marina, remembers tying up between two of the many standing trees on Table Rock. A lantern would be hung from the tree at each end of the boat. Using live minnows, they took lots of crappie attracted by the lights.

The majority of fishermen in the first few years of Table Rock still fished with live bait. Anglers could boat a short distance and tie up to one of the many trees still standing in the coves and flooded creeks. Crappie were the most frequently caught fish using live minnows or worms. Undoubtably, other species were caught by crappie fishermen. Live or natural baits are very effective and large numbers of game fish were taken on Table Rock in the 60's using this method. However, as the decade passed, changes in the lake and more importantly, changes in angling attitudes began to alter fishing techniques. By the end of the 1960's, casting artificial lures was the preferred method.

Articles and stories about bass fishing on Table Rock during the early years indicate that bass were fairly easy to catch. There was no size limit on black bass and the daily limit was ten fish per angler. It is obvious from the stories and photographs of this era that most fishermen did very well and kept most of the fish they caught. Throughout the 60's, bass fishing grew in popularity. The following story about Norton Dablemont excerpted from Ridge Runner by Larry Dablemont gives some idea of how the bass fishery was developing.[19]

"On Easter Sunday of 1966, I went farther up Long Creek than I had ever fished, way past Clevenger Cove to a place where an old roadbed went across the lake. The lake was rising and fairly muddy because a big rain had come before a cold front and we had arrived at the tail end of it. It was cold that day and it would snow awhile, then rain awhile, then sleet awhile and then the clouds would break for awhile. Carl Emmick was catching some crappie from the boat and so I got out and began to wade out onto that old road bed where some logs and rootwads had floated up. I got up on top of a log to make a cast and a big bass picked up the jig and eel I was using and moved away with it. I set the hook hard, lost my footing and came off the log as the bass headed for deeper water. That time, the bass had the better footing but I got ahold of myself and finally got a good breath or two after the shock of the cold water. My bass was still on and she fought like a champion. I worked her around the logs and back toward the bank, finally pulling her out onto that old roadbed.

The folks back at Three Oaks were really excited and they went about getting the bass officially weighed and fluoroscoped to be sure it had no lead added to it. I got into some dry clothes and got warmed up and signed all the papers and affadavits as to how and where it had been caught. It tipped the scales at ten pounds, four ounces, and I'll be darned if it didn't wind up being the biggest largemouth registered in Missouri in 1966, winning first place. The results were published in Sports Afield at the end of the year. I got a pin of some kind from the magazine and a new rod and reel with a lot of lures and other fishing equipment. And the resort gave me a weeks stay free of charge the following spring. Velma and I started fishing there every time we had a few days free and she caught her biggest bass in Clevenger Cove in 1967, eight pounds, six ounces."

During the 60's on Table Rock, fishing boats were small simple craft. The average boat was a 14-16 ft. aluminum V-bottom with a small engine of 25 hp. or less. Some boats were still paddled by hand or used early stern-mount trolling motors. The wooden john-boat was still used, but aluminum models were becoming more common. Small fiberglass run-abouts were seen on the lake as well.

With the limited range of boats and the large amount of visible cover on the lake, most Table Rock anglers traveled short distances. Often it was only necessary to tie up to a tree and fish. Anchors were also used to cast or still fish in a given area.

During the first years of Table Rock, fishing boats did not develop very much. Most anglers seemed content to catch fish from whatever craft was available. Based on the number of fish caught in these early years, this is understandable. Near the end of the decade, the bass boat became a reality. Made in both aluminum and fiberglass, the bass boat began to incorporate features that made fishing more comfortable and more efficient. The advent of organized fishing tournaments in the late 60's rapidly accelerated this trend.

Tournament fishing on Table Rock during the 60's consisted of small club events. Charlie Campbell of Forsyth helped start the Ozarks Bass Club out of Springfield in the mid-60's. This group of about 50 anglers was probably the first bass club in Missouri. They held several competitions on Table Rock complete with shotgun starts and weigh-ins. Charlie recalls part of the fun was the take-off and race to "honey holes" with outboards up to 75 hp. There were no aerated livewells at this time. Lots of good bass were caught with competitors often limiting out with ten fish. Largemouth were by far the species most often brought in. Some fish were released and some were cleaned and donated to charity. The popularity of club tournaments grew rapidly and groups were organized in many cities around Table Rock. Often these clubs would compete against each other.

Dave Barker of Branson graduated from the School of the Ozarks in 1961 and began fishing Table Rock regularly in 1965. He remembers the lake as having lots of flooded trees and brush and fairly good color. Dave mostly fished the lower end of the reservoir in Long Creek and the White just above the dam. Largemouth bass and crappie were abundant. He also caught white bass and trot lined for catfish. The majority of anglers on Table Rock in the early years used live bait, but Dave has always preferred artificials.

He bought his first Ambassador reel in 1965 and began using plastic worms extensively. He recollects some people making their own worms from strips of rubber inner tubes. He also used a Mitchell 300 spinning reel, Zebco 33 or 66 reels, fiberglass rods and monofilament line.

During the 1960's, Dave Barker began refining his fishing skills on "the Rock". He used the jig-and-frog or jig-and-eel successfully on quality bass up to six pounds. He used crankbaits like the Bomber, a popular wooden plug with a brass bill. He also remembers the Rapala being rented around the lake for about $20 each with a $20 deposit. In 1968, he bought a 16 ft. Richline aluminum boat with an 18 hp. Evinrude and a Silvertroll trolling motor. This was a major step in this angler's journey to become one of the most successful anglers on Table Rock.

Table Rock has always attracted fishermen from the local area as well as from Missouri, the mid-west and the entire country. Early on, some locals fished from the shore or used johnboats. Visitors to the lake often came to fish, but many did not own a boat. Some brought an outboard. Most resorts supplied a fishing boat with their rooms or rented boats. The typical resort fishing craft was a 14 ft. aluminum model fitted with a 10 to 15 horsepower motor. Trolling motors were rare at this time. Some vacationers brought early fiber-glass runabouts.

It is hard to imagine now, but in the early years, many of the coves on Table Rock Lake were full of standing timber. The smaller boats used were well suited to these conditions. It was often only necessary to tie up to any available tree and fish in- place for crappie or bass. The run-and -gun technique of today was years in the future.

The period of 1958 to 1970 was a nostalgic period on Table Rock. The reservoir that had been built primarily for flood control was becoming a world renowned fishery. For the most part, fishing was very good on Table Rock during its first decade. The lake was becoming a desirable fishing destination for anglers from all across the country and particularly in the mid-west region. About 20% of Table Rock's anglers were local and about 25% were from out-of-state. The rest came from other areas of Missouri.

Articles about fishing success on Table Rock were showing up in all regional newspapers and in national magazines. The deep, clean water, the miles of rocky shoreline and the rugged beauty of the surrounding Ozarks provided an irresistible call to the anglers and vacationers of America. Developments of the late 60's and early 70's would increase this attraction. Table Rock would both benefit and suffer from its beauty.

Harold Ensley and J.D. Fletcher

Jim Reeves with two nice Table Rock bass

Chapter 7
The 70's

The decade of the 1970's brought momentous changes to Table Rock Lake. The lake was developing a national reputation as one of the best bass fisheries in the country. This brought increasing numbers of visitors and fishermen to the area. Cities like Branson, Kimberling City, Cape Fair, Shell Knob and Eagle Rock were developing rapidly as both vacation and retirement destinations. The number of resorts had increased significantly around Table Rock.

During this decade, lake levels varied from a low of 897 ft. in March of 1977 to a high of 928 ft. reached in April of '73 and June of '74. Within each year, the water levels seldom varied more than 10 or 12 feet.

Fishing tournaments became a way of life for Table Rock. Angling equipment and methods advanced significantly. The bass boat grew up with this lake and grew in size and sophistication throughout the 70's. Angling remained very good on Table Rock, but the fishery was under assault by increasingly numerous and adept fishers.

The Missouri Department of Conservation responded by studying the lake, the anglers and the fish. As a result of these studies, new regulations were enacted and some stocking programs were initiated. The 1970's were the glory days of fishing on Table Rock. Everyone wanted to fish here and it seems like just about everyone did.

Two events in the late 60's were to have a significant impact on bass fishing and Table Rock Lake. In 1967, Ray Scott organized the All-American Invitational bass tournament on Beaver Lake and in

1968, Forrest Wood began building Ranger bass boats. Scott would go on to found B.A.S.S. (Bass Anglers Sportsman Society), Bassmaster magazine and the BASS Masters Classic. This organization did more than any other to promote tournament style bass fishing and the sport in general. B.A.S.S. can be credited with many advances in fishing including catch-and-release, well organized weigh-ins, the required use of life jackets and kill switches and the organization of bass anglers into an effective lobbying bloc for the sport.

Ranger Boats, a long-time sponsor of B.A.S.S. tournaments, made significant contributions to the design, styling, performance and safety of the bass boat. As the sport of bass fishing developed, Ranger and many other manufacturers began producing boats which increasingly improved the effectiveness of anglers. Faster designs, modern livewells, expansive storage, casting decks, bow-mount trolling motors and depth finders are just some of the improvements that gained widespread use during the decade of the 70's.

Another individual who helped grow the sport of fishing, particularly on Table Rock, was Springfieldian Johnny Morris. Johnny, an avid bass fisherman, began selling lures and tackle from his father's liquor store in 1971. In 1972, he founded Bass Pro Shop. His fishing tackle store would develop into one of the largest tackle and outdoors retailers in the world. Bass Pro Shop became a destination for anglers heading to Table Rock from all over the country. In 1974, Bass Pro premiered their catalog. This helped make available to large numbers of fishermen, the growing assortment of fishing tackle, particularly equipment suitable for bassin' on Table Rock and other southwest Missouri impoundments. Tracker Boats were introduced in 1978. These inexpensive, aluminum craft made bass boats available to a wider audience of anglers. Tracker boats came as a complete fishing package including motor, trailer, depth finder, trolling motor and livewell.

The explosion of fishing technology and interest in the 1970's put pressure on the Table Rock fishery. Anglers were becoming more adept at catching all species of fish under a variety of conditions and depths and throughout the year.

To assure the continued strength of the Table Rock fishery, the Missouri Department of Conservation initiated several projects on the lake in the 70's. In 1976, a size limit of 10 inches and a daily limit of 10 fish were placed on crappie in the James River area.

Colvin[20] reported the reason for these changes was to reduce the harvest of one and two year old crappie. This would allow more fish to grow to a larger size. At this time, the size and possession limit changes were only imposed on the highly pressured James River arm.

Wide variations in yearly recruitment or reproductive success for crappie would result in the 10 in. size limit being imposed lakewide in 1984. Crappie fishing success seemed to have deteriorated since the lake's early days and has never returned to those high catch rates of the early 60's.

Walleye were stocked in Table Rock in 1974 by the Department of Conservation. About 2000 8" fingerlings and 450,000 fry were introduced into the lake. Since there were no more stockings in this decade, it is doubtful that this introduction was able to establish a viable population.

Paddlefish were stocked in Table Rock Lake throughout the 1970's. Although it would take years for this fishery to develop, this was an important program for the lake. Paddlefish populations throughout the United States had been decimated due primarily to habitat loss as a result of dam building.

Graham[21] reported that the stocking of paddlefish fry and fingerlings into Table Rock was the first major attempt to introduce these fish into previously unoccupied waters.

In 1970, paddlefish fry (about ¼ inch long) were released in the James River. From 1972 through 1977, there were annual stockings of fingerlings (10-12 inches long). 25,000 fingerlings were released in 1973 and 38,000 in 1974. A total of 83,000 fingerlings were introduced into the James arm during the six year period.

Subsequent population samples never revealed any spoonbill from the 1970 stocking. The smaller fry were probably eaten by larger predatory fish. The fingerlings released did well, though. The paddlefish population showed good growth rates which were enhanced by the long growing season and abundant food supply of this area.

Beginning in 1976, the 15 inch limit on all black bass was initiated on Table Rock. The creel limit for bass was lowered from a daily limit of ten to six in 1978. These new restrictions were the result of extensive study by the Department of Conservation. It was hoped that the new rules would protect the younger bass and allow more to grow to a larger size and maturity. This would mean more fish would spawn and lead to a more sustainable population. It would also result in more quality fish. A 15 inch bass typically weighs about two pounds.

These regulations were imposed based upon creel surveys and electrofishing studies done on Table Rock throughout the 1970's. As noted during the 60's, there was increasing interest and fishing pressure on the black basses. Catch-and-release was not widely practiced. You only have to look at photographs from this era to see that most anglers kept their catch.

The comprehensive creel surveys done by Hanson[22] during the 60's were continued in the years 1970-1972. Hanson's report[23] for these years covered surveys done on Long Creek and the James River. This study was performed spring through fall only, as at that time less than 5% of the fishing was done during the winter (December- February).

The fishing pressure remained fairly steady during the first three years of the 70's. Crappie fishing remained good in the James, but fell off in Long Creek. Black bass fishing remained good in both areas with largemouth continuing to account for about 80% of this species caught. Smallmouth made up an insignificant part of the creel. In both of these arms studied, largemouth, crappie, white bass and bluegill made up over 75% of the total fish counted.

The number of white bass caught rose considerably when compared to the late 60's. Particularly in 1971, large numbers of whites were taken in the James and Long Creek. Channel catfish were also taken in good numbers.

During this study, the lake level rarely rose above power pool, but did not fall below 900' either. Secchi readings in the James averaged about five feet while in Long Creek, they averaged almost eleven feet. The James was developing as a productive fishery, heavily laden with nutrients. These nutrients supported a healthy population of shad which contributed to a strong bass population. Long Creek was also a good bass fishery, but did not receive the fishing pressure or publicity that the James area did.

Gary Novinger[24] did an extensive study of the bass population on Table Rock from 1973 to 1983. The primary purpose of this study was to determine the impact of the 15 inch limit on black bass. The study was carried out on James River and Long Creek. The work relied heavily on electrofishing results, but also used creel surveys.

Novinger reported three reasons for selecting the 15 inch limit: the apparent self-imposed decision by most anglers to release bass less than 12", the intent to protect black bass up to a size capable of eating gizzard shad and allowing bass to take advantage of their good growth rates for a longer period. It was hoped the 15 inch limit would increase the harvest rate to one fish every four hours fished and the catch rate to one bass every two hours.[25]

Electrofishing is a technique used by fishery biologists to sample fish populations. This method is typically done from a specially designed boat equipped with electrified chains hanging down into the water from a rack at the bow and bright spot lights. The crew usually consists of three or four people. One pilots the boat, one collects data and one or two net fish. Electrofishing is almost always done at night during the spawn when fish are shallow and more susceptible to capture. The boat is maneuvered into spawning areas along the bank in coves. When the chains are electrified, fish within a certain diameter are stunned. The netters capture the shocked fish and transfer them to the data collector. This person identifies the species, measures the fish, collects a scale sample in some cases, releases the fish and records the data.

Electrofishing is most successful, at least for most fresh water game fish, when done at night. For scientific purposes, it is important to perform these studies at about the same time each year and in the same locations. This method is effective in obtaining an acceptable sample of fish for comparative studies. Although physically challenging, electrofishing is a relatively simple and inexpensive way to gather data. Fish are not harmed by this technique.

Electrofishing does have its drawbacks. It relies on choosing the best time of year and best locations to obtain good representative samples. High water conditions often interfere as fish may be harder to locate and may be spawning too deep to capture. Poor water clarity may make it difficult to see the fish. Largemouth bass, crappie and bluegill are probably best sampled by electrofishing. Kentucky and smallmouth bass tend to spawn deeper and therefore may be more difficult to shock. Other fishes like walleye and white bass tend to spawn in the upper ends of streams and creeks making accessibility more difficult. Electrofishing also provides no information on anglers, fishing techniques or harvest rates. Creel surveys give a much broader view of a particular fishery. Nevertheless, electrofishing has become the preferred method for collecting information on most game fish populations on Table Rock. It is an effective, efficient technique for gathering comparative data.

The black bass populations in the James and Long Creek were good, but varied considerably during the period. It was becoming apparent that fishing effort and harvest were only one part of the determinant of fish populations. Spawning success, water levels, predation and food supply also had a large impact on the number of fish in Table Rock. Many factors were going into the availability of game fish for angling purposes.

The years 1968, 1970, 1971 and 1973 were excellent years for largemouth bass reproduction. The following four years (1974-77) saw poor recruitment. Better spawning occurred in 1978, 1979 and 1981. Spotted bass had an almost opposite trend with good spawns in 1969, 1974, 1977 and 1978.[26]

Largemouth bass grow to 15 inches between the ages of three and four years. Kentuckies reach this length between four and five years. Growth rates are most influenced by available food and the length of the growing season. Mature bass in Table Rock eat primarily shad (gizzard and threadfin), aquatic invertebrates and crawfish. The relative abundance of these food sources, particularly shad, has an important effect on bass growth and numbers.

Table Rock has a good population of gizzard shad. Gizzard shad do not grow as fast here, probably due to the lower average productivity and greater depth of the water. Bass and crappie will eat gizzard shad which are up to one year old. Older shad become too large for successful predation. With a slower growth rate on Table Rock, these baitfish provide an important food source for the gamefish.

Threadfin shad are smaller (rarely exceeding 6") than gizzard shad and therefore provide a good continuous food source. Threadfin entered Table Rock from existing populations in Lake Springfield and stockings by the Arkansas Game and Fish Commission in Long Creek and Beaver Lake. They are well established and can be seen in huge schools throughout the lake. One drawback is that being pelagic (preferring deep water), they may tend to draw gamefish into deeper water making them harder to catch.

Both threadfin and gizzard shad will experience winter kills on Table Rock. Threadfin typically do not survive in water below 50 degrees F. However, the large populations observed throughout the year on Table Rock indicate they have managed to do so. They may find warmer water locations near springs in the winter or perhaps they have evolved to become more tolerant. It is also possible that by hybridizing with gizzard shad, the threadfin have become less cold temperature sensitive.

Novinger[27] reported that the 15 inch limit increased the total numbers of bass in Table Rock. It did not appear to increase the amount of fish over 15 inches in the lake. Whether due to changes in attitude or the length limit, more anglers were releasing bass. On the James during this study (1973-1983), the percentage of anglers keeping one bass fell from 41 to 18%. There were similar results on Long Creek.

One other interesting detail from Novinger's study comes from the tagged fish results. Returned tags from captured fish indicate that there were good numbers of bass over 17 inches being caught. The tag study also showed that it becomes increasingly harder to catch bass as they increase in size. The percentage of returned tags declined steadily as the size of the bass increased.

The Missouri Department of Conservation deserves considerable recognition for the amount of effort and study they committed to Table Rock Lake. The data they generated helped us all understand the fishery better. The carefully studied regulations and programs established during the seventies had a positive impact on Table Rock fish, particularly bass, crappie and paddlefish. Their work also helped shape the attitudes of anglers on this lake and fisheries across the country.

The sport of fishing was growing like a big fish in a little pond. Tackle was developed for all types of fish and fishing. High quality, level-wind reels with backlash control became more popular and affordable. The Ambassador 5000, although available since the 50's, became a mainstay in most serious fishermen's arsenals. Stronger graphite rods introduced by Shakespeare and Fenwick gave anglers the ability to cast far and accurately and feel what was on their line. Special rods were available for crappie, walleye and catfish. Bass fishermen could choose from rods and reels designed specifically for plastic worms, crankbaits or spoons. Lightweight spinning outfits made for small, soft plastic baits were well suited to the deep, clear waters of Table Rock Reservoir. Quality monofilament line was used almost exclusively now. It was strong and flexible and worked well on all types of tackle.

Basic tackle was offered in a wide assortment. Hooks specifically designed for worms and other soft plastics were available. Some came with built-in weed guards. Cone-shaped slip sinkers became popular with the Texas-rig. Monofilament line presented a much wider assortment of line tests.

In the 1970's, the technique of flipping was developed on lakes like Table Rock by pros like Basil Bacon and Dee Thomas. Flipping involves a long stout rod of seven to eight feet and a large baitcast reel with heavy monofilament line.

The flipping technique employs a method of swinging a bait into a specific location using the rod as a lever. The flipper typically works very close to heavy cover and drops his bait into openings around vegetation, trees or docks. Baits are usually large jigs with plastic or natural trailers or soft plastics like worms and lizards. The flipping technique allows an angler to work along a bank with heavy cover and target every specific fishy location. When a hook-up is made, the heavy tackle allows the fish to be horsed from the cover. This technique was better suited to the areas of Table Rock with darker water and more visible cover. The James, the Kings and Long Creek probably saw most of this approach on the lake.

Structure fishing began to be used by more fishermen in this decade. In broad terms, structure can refer to any change in water conditions, lake bed topography or cover. Serious anglers have always considered these elements when fishing. Some probed the depths with heavy lures to "feel" the changes in contours and locate cover. In the modern era of fishing, structure became most associated with underwater contour changes like points, humps and channels. The introduction of depth finders and contour maps made locating and fishing these areas easier. Table Rock was particularly well- suited to this approach with its deep water and variety of contours. With increasing fishing pressure and reduced visible cover, this style of angling began to attract the attention of serious fishermen, especially guides and tournament competitors.

Dan Langley of Shell Knob has studied Table Rock and its fishes' behavior since the 60's. An early proponent of structure fishing, Dan developed his own maps of the lake through many hours of fishing and watching his "Little Green Box" flasher. Through the 70's, Dan structure fished in 15-25' of water using plastic worms and early spinnerbaits like the Agitator. This was considered "deep" fishing at the time.

Over the years, Langley has progressively fished even deeper using spoons, jigs and large spinnerbaits. Like many other anglers, he expanded his fishing to include more night and winter outings.

Some of the changes Dan has adapted to on Table Rock are reduced visible cover, higher average water levels and a perceived change in bass' preference for shad over crawfish. This fisherman's in-depth study of the black bass has enabled him to have many very successful days and tournaments on Table Rock. He has two Table Rock bass over 9 lbs., one caught on a tandem spinnerbait and one on a 3 J jigging spoon.

Although many lures were successfully used on the Rock in the 70's, the most successful has to be the plastic worm. Since its widespread use began in the 60's, the plastic worm has probably been responsible for more and bigger bass than any other lure. An angler using Texas-rigged six to eight inch worms was almost guaranteed to catch bass on Table Rock. As the decade passed, the plastic worm began a metamorphosis. The worm changed colors, changed sizes and grew all kinds of appendages. The jig-and-pig was widely used on the lake. Originally, this combination bait consisted of a fairly large jig (¼ to ⅝ oz.) and an Uncle Josh Pork Frog (thus the pig). The jig-and-pig developed a reputation as a big fish bait and certainly accounted for many lunker largemouth. J.D. Fletcher's biggest largemouth, an eight pounder, was caught on a jig-and-pig in the early 60's. This bait would also develop with numerous styles of jigs and trailers used. Eventually, most bass anglers would opt for plastic trailers, probably due in part to the cost and mess of the natural version.

Topwater plugs have been a mainstay on the rivers of Table Rock since before the lake was impounded. The early float trips on the James and White often saw anglers chunking large wooden baits like the Lucky 13, Bass-Oreno and Ding Bat. On the big water, fishermen liked to use baits like Arbogast's Jitterbug and Hula Popper. Table Rock fishermen have more recently employed surface lures like the Devil's Horse, Zara Spook or Woodwalker. These lures required special presentations and could be worked slow on top to aggravate big fish. Some anglers refined their skill to be able to keep these baits in the same area for an extended period. Whatever the skill of the caster, topwaters accounted for some exciting action.

The 70's saw the introduction of the buzzbait. The Lunker Lure was the first topwater bait of this design. Whether over flats, along bluffs or through standing timber, the buzzbait gained a reputation for catching lots of bass under the right conditions on Table Rock.

The spinnerbait has been around in some configuration for over a hundred years. What this style of lure always has is a spinning blade. The spinnerbait in its present safety pin design came into widespread use during the 1970's. The spinnerbait is a very versatile lure. It can be fished fast on top creating a wake. It can be slow rolled along the bottom or over cover. Spinnerbaits can be "helicoptered" down on dropoffs or bumped past trees. This bait is almost weedless. It is very effective in the spring, but can be used year-round on Table Rock.

During the 70's, spinnerbaits became available in multiple sizes, styles and colors. The three main types of spinnerbait blades are the Colorado, Indiana and willow leaf. They come with single blades or combinations up to three. Two basic styles are the short-arm and long-arm. The long-arm hook extends farther back and has better hooking capability, but also hangs up more. The short-arm can be worked more effectively around cover.

In this decade, spinnerbait skirts were made of plastic or rubber. Generally used in sizes from ¼ to ⅝ oz., some anglers began dressing these baits with a pork or plastic trailer. Tandem blades were popular with varying combinations of Colorado and willow leafs. Large willow leafs were particularly effective in the spring and fall.

As is often the case, anglers developed certain preferences for color, style and presentation on this lake. In addition to its common uses, Table Rock fishermen developed a special technique used on deep bluffs. Anglers made long casts with Colorado bladed spinnerbaits perpendicular to steep banks. The bait was retrieved quickly back to the boat creating a wake on the surface. This method produced good numbers of spotted bass even during the heat of summer. For some reason, this technique lost its effectiveness and is seldom used today.

A wide assortment of crankbaits were used on Table Rock throughout the seventies. Bomber Bait Co. made a crawdad imitator that worked well on the rocky shorelines. The Bomber's tie-on was on a large metal lip which gave the bait an erratic action. Bagley, Rebel and other manufacturers produced popular billed crankbaits modeled after the Big O. This fat-bodied diver was originally hand carved by Fred Young. Its popularity led to the development of many alphabet style plugs still used today. The Hellbender and Martin Lizard were used effectively as bottom diggers. Bill Anderson who is now with the Missouri Department of Conservation caught a 7 lb. 9 oz. bass on a Hellbender in 1965 fishing near Indian Point. Creek Chub's Flatfish and Kautsky's Lazy Ike had good action for bass. In addition to its still often used minnow bait, Rapala introduced several realistic crankbait models that ran at different depths. Crankbaits were being offered in a wider assortment of colors.

Lures like the Rogue became very specialized weapons. As discussed in Chapter 6, fishermen like Ralph Lambert developed modifications which made the stickbait a particularly effective lure on Table Rock. Weighted Rogues and similar plugs were twitched down to suspend around cedar trees. Especially in the pre-spawn period of February through April, this method could produce monster bass. This bass angling approach generated the development of various sizes, depths and colors of stickbaits. Although not exclusively attributed to Table Rock, twitching a suspending jerkbait is often associated with this lake's reputation.

Another method which started seeing expanded use during the 70's was deep spooning. Although one of the most primitive lures in design, the spoon can be credited with large catches of all the basses. The first fishing spoon was created by J.T. Buel in 1840 and was crafted from an actual table spoon. In the first half of the 20th century, spoons were often fairly sophisticated baits like the ones produced by Al Foss. In the 50's and 60's, the simpler Johnson spoon with or without a trailer became a mainstay of many structure fishermen on Table Rock. The Dixie Jet Flutter Spoon was used successfully as a casting spoon. Spooning in water up to 100 ft. was well suited to the deep, clear water of this lake.

Many Table Rock anglers used smaller baits on spinning or spincast outfits. Lures like the Beetle Spin and Road Runner were effective on black bass, white bass and crappie. Small leadhead jigs worked well for crappie off docks, in brush piles and around standing timber. Some bass anglers also began to use small jigs dressed with plastic grubs. In the clear water areas of Table Rock, fishermen were finding these smaller baits fished with light line on structure could take good numbers of bass.

Natural bait continued to be popular, especially for crappie, bluegill and catfish. Some anglers used large gizzard shad hooked through the back fin and fished on a controlled line to catch large bass.

Bait shops sold lots of minnows, crawdads, nightcrawlers, river worms and crickets. However, the reduction in the crappie populations and changes in attitudes toward bass fishing techniques began to reduce the demand for live bait. The trend away from live bait and to artificials continued.

As angling techniques advanced and the number of lures multiplied, the need for better tackle boxes arose. The toolbox type of tackle box made from wood, metal or plastic no longer met the needs of some serious fishermen on Table Rock. Larger boxes with different sized storage compartments were demanded. Anglers were now carrying a wide assortment of crankbaits, spinnerbaits, jigs and soft plastic baits in addition to terminal tackle and other equipment. They wanted boxes with special compartments for crankbaits and topwaters, racks for spinnerbaits and separate modules for worms. The tendency for soft plastic baits to melt and adhere to other tackle prompted the development of the wormproof tackle box. During the 70's, tackle boxes got larger and more sophisticated.

Bass tournaments became a way of life on Table Rock Reservoir during the 1970's. Table Rock had gained a reputation for bass in both quantity and quality. In the 60's, tournaments were usually loosely organized events. They were often held by small fishing clubs, businesses, civic organizations or just a group of friends. There were no restrictions other than the Missouri regulations. There was no length limit on bass and the daily limit was ten fish. Boats were simpler craft, usually aluminum fishing boats with low horsepower motors. Despite the relative low-tech tackle and equipment, large numbers of fish were caught and usually kept. Dave Barker recalls a tournament held in the mid-60's. As an employee of the School of the Ozarks, he assisted with the weighin. He says he remembers several barrels full of fish collected at the weigh-in. Most of these bass were donated to local charities.

By the early seventies, tournament fishing was developing into a well organized, popular sport. Advances in tackle, boats and methods increased anglers' ability to fish competitively. The influence of B.A.S.S. was widespread and helped create considerable interest in competitive fishing. B.A.S.S. held two tournaments on Table Rock in the early 70's. In 1970, Bill Dance won a B.A.S.S. event held in November with 52 lbs. 6 oz. In April of 1971, John

Powell won their event with 59 lbs. 13 oz.

Arvil Ming[28] of the Missouri Department of Conservation studied bass tournaments in Missouri from March 1974 to March 1975. Ming's report reveals the extent to which tournament fishing had developed and the amount of interest in Table Rock as a bass fishery. This study documented 506 national, regional, open and club tournaments. 11,435 anglers participated, catching 24,502 bass and releasing 65% of the catch. The average catch rate was one bass for every 5 ¼ hours fished. Of the 44 national, regional and open tourneys held that year, 18 or 41% were held on Table Rock. 30% of the state's club events were held on Table Rock.

The National Bass Federation sponsored a national tournament on Table Rock during this study and the Mid-America Bass Fishermen's Association (the largest bass fishing organization in Missouri with 1000 members) held three regional events. There were several open tourneys held by a variety of clubs, businesses and organizations. The number of anglers in the larger events varied from 20 to 202. The smaller bass fishing clubs averaged about 17 contestants at their outings. The anglers fishing Table Rock generally had good success.

Tournament fishermen were becoming much more conservation minded. Almost all tournaments imposed length limits of at least 12 inches. Some used 15 inch limits. Weigh-in limits varied from five fish per angler to the state regulation of ten. Livewells were becoming more common and were required in some of the larger events. Catch-and- release was widely practiced. In this study, 65% of all fish weighed-in were released alive. A comparison creel survey done on Table Rock during the same period as Ming's study showed non-tournament anglers released only 17% of bass.

This project sponsored by the Missouri Department of Conservation captured the changing environment of fishing in general and bass fishing in particular. Bass fishing was becoming a highly evolved technical sport with more and more concern about conservation. Ming concluded his report by stating that there was no evidence that bass tournaments were harming the fishery and no need for special regulations on these events.

The bass boat developed in an interdependent relationship with bass tournaments. Improvements in boat design, equipment and speed changed the way anglers fished for bass. The rules and arrangements of tournaments influenced how bass boats were developed.

Some of the improvements in fishing boats during the 70's were console steering, raised, carpeted casting decks, bow-mounted trolling motors, aerated livewells, rod and storage compartments, depth finders and high performance engines. These changes made fishing more comfortable, safer and efficient.

One of the most important tools of the tournament angler is the depth finder. Carl Lowrance of Joplin, Missouri produced one of the first sonar units for freshwater fishing in 1957. It sold for $150. In 1959, Lowrance premiered the "Little Green Box", a portable depth finder. More than a million of these units were produced from 1959-1984. In 1974, this company released their first graph recorder. It was a combination flasher and paper chart. Lowrance retains a reputation as a producer of quality sonar gear. The Humminbird flasher was a standard on many fishing boats. Early portable models progressed to gimball mounts and eventually liquid crystal technology. Chart recorders were so revolutionary at this time, that Minnesota proposed a law to ban them. In 1977, Lowrance introduced a pH meter based on research by Dr. Loren Hill. Although based on valid science, this device never really took off.

The trolling motor has seen numerous improvements over the years. The basic stern-mount, hand controlled trolling motor like the SilverTrol had been around since the 1930's. In 1961, G.H. Harris invented the first foot control model, the Guide-Rite. This model eventually became the MotorGuide. Stan Sloan, winner of Ray Scott's All American Invitational bass tournament on Beaver Lake in 1967, is recognized as one of the first fishermen to mount his trolling motor on the bow. He is quoted as asking, "Is it easier to push a chain or pull a chain?"

The Electro Pal was a popular trolling motor with guides on Table Rock. A 12 volt stern-mount, it had forward and reverse and several speeds. With an Electro Pal, a guide could maneuver an aluminum fishing boat from the stern through the heavily timbered coves.

In the early 70's, MotorGuide introduced the first retractable bow-mount trolling motor. These units had variable speed and would become the standard for all future designs. By 1975, trollers had up to 24 pounds of thrust available from 12/24 volt (two battery) systems. More power allowed bass boats to grow bigger.

Special equipment was also developed to meet the growing popularity of night fishing for bass, crappie and catfish. In addition to lanterns and spot lights, the Moon Glow light, when attached to the side of the boat, provided illumination for casting.

The bass boat developed from a wide range of influences. One of the forerunners in fishing craft was Skeeter Boats. Skeeter produced a boat in 1948 specifically designed for fishing. It was a fairly small boat of about 14 ft. built of molded marine plywood with a flat bottom and a streamlined bow. This shape would become the precursor for future bass boats. Skeeter was an innovator in fishing boat production, introducing fiberglass hulls in the 1950's and stick-steered, 15 ft. tri-hulled boats in the 60's. In the 70's, Skeeter had the first V-bottom bass boat and the first model rated for 150 hp.

Charlie Campbell, well-known professional angler from Forsyth, Missouri remembers the first fiberglass bass boat he ever saw. Charlie was working as a guide out of Devil's Pool Resort near Long Creek. Some time in the mid-60's, another local guide purchased a fishing boat made by Kinsey Craft of Flippin, Arkansas. The boat was a 16 ft. fiberglass model with a small tiller-controlled outboard. Charlie says they called these craft "guide boats". Later on, they added a front swivel seat mounted on a large fiberglass pedestal and a non-aerated livewell.

Ranger Boats is almost synonymous with tournament angling. Since the early seventies, Ranger has supplied boats for the BASS Masters Classic. Forest Wood, founder of Ranger, continually refined his fishing boats to meet the needs of fishermen. From the stubby blunt-nosed models of the early seventies to today's sleek V-hulls, Ranger has refined its boats for performance, safety and fishability. Ranger's close association with B.A.S.S. and their commitment to angler input resulted in refinements to handling, storage, livewells, comfort and eye-catching finishes.

Tournament fishing demanded quick hole shots, high speed and stable running. Prop designs and outboard position were modified to achieve fast start-ups and good high-end performance. With motors peaking out at 150 hp., hull designs were developed for pad running on plane. Hulls were also designed to reduce porpoising and chine walking.

Charlie Campbell came to this area in 1958 as Forsyth High School's basketball coach. He immediately began fishing Bull Shoals, Taneycomo and the newly created Table Rock Lake. During the summer, Charlie guided on all three area lakes.

When Table Rock was completed and began releasing 45 degree water downstream, it forever changed Taneycomo from a warm water bass and crappie fishery to a trout haven. The upper end of Bull Shoals was also affected by the colder water and variable flows. White bass fishing declined, but walleye angling improved on Bull Shoals below Taneycomo.

Charlie often guided fishing enthusiasts out of Devil's Pool Resort. In the early years, he used small wooden fishing boats propelled by handmade wooden paddles. Later on, aluminum boats with 25 hp. motors were used and hand-controlled stern-mount trolling motors were added. Charlie remembers sitting on top of the "big motor" and steering the trolling motor with his foot. Using an Ambassador 5000 with early monofilament on a fiberglass rod, he lead his clients to consistently catch their ten fish limit.

In the sixties, there was still lots of visible timber in Table Rock. Campbell says it was not uncommon to tie up to a tree and catch a limit of fish in one location on plastic worms. These baits were typically flip tail worms, 7-10 inches. At first, anglers hooked them through the head with an exposed hook, but this often resulted in snagging. Area anglers began using weed guards, sometimes made by inserting plastic broom straws into a lead head jig. Later, the Texas-rig was adopted.

Charlie Campbell is well known for his topwater skill. Particularly during the spring and summer, he took many Table Rock bass on baits like the Crippled Killer, Creek Chub Darter and Zara Spook. His passion for on-top fishing inspired him to develop the Woodwalker bait.

Campbell starting fishing professional tournaments in the early 70's. He quit teaching in 1973 and started on the B.A.S.S. tour in 1974. He has been a consistent supporter of fishery and conservation efforts. Experiencing a decline in bass fishing on Table Rock in the mid-seventies, Charlie was a vocal promoter of catch-and-release, six fish limits and the 15 inch length limit. He continues to champion fishing in this area through his conservation and educational work.

"Table Rock is one of the best tournament lakes in the country," says Campbell. With all the different areas, types of cover, water depths and clarities available within a relatively easy boat ride, Table Rock offers many opportunities for various styles and patterns. One of Charlie's best fishing results came in a National Bass Club Federation tournament in the early 70's on Table Rock. Fishing in the finals on the last day, he was catching good fish on a Spook and a Rebel follow-up bait. Up the James, he hooked a hefty largemouth with an unusual spot on its side. The fish got off, but two hours later, Charlie came back and boated the same fish on a Balsa B. Heading back, Charlie stopped in a cove near Joe Bald. An errant cast sent his Spook up into a tree. The bait fell out and a five pound bass nailed it. His catch helped propel Missouri to a victory in this event.

In 1996, Campbell fished the B.A.S.S. Missouri Invitational on Table Rock. Dealing with changing April weather and a cold front, Charlie fought through two broken ribs and pneumonia to finish second place.

Charlie Campbell is an excellent example of the dedicated anglers who fish this impoundment. He has passed on his love for Table Rock to fishing partners like President George Bush, Senator Kit Bond, Ray Scott, Johnny Morris and Shoji Tabuchi. Charlie is a member of the Living Legends of American Sport Fishing and was recently inducted into the Missouri Sports Hall of Fame.

Wallace Lea has fished Bull Shoals and Table Rock extensively since 1963. Early on, Wallace fished the James River area from shore and by boat. He liked to fly fish, but also used a Pfleuger baitcaster on a steel rod. He became a master at using many baits like the Bomber crankbaits, the jig-and-pig and spinnerbaits. He replaced the in-line spinners of the 60's with the safety pin style in the 70's. Lea saw good results with early models like the Tarantula popularized by Virgil Ward. One of Lea's best days came in the early seventies in the Long Creek area of Table Rock. Using a jig-and-eel, he caught six bass weighing 34 lbs., including his biggest largemouth of 9 lbs.10 oz.

Wallace refined his understanding of this fishery through spending an average 200 days a year on the water. He was one of the first anglers to develop structure fishing on these waters. His observations during low water conditions prompted him to target channel swings, tree lines and humps. He doesn't really prefer deep fishing, but found this trend necessary as the lake changed over time. He feels the introduction of threadfin shad into Table Rock tended to move the black bass deeper in search of this open water baitfish. He also believes fish become bait sensitive forcing fishermen to constantly reevaluate their lures and presentations.

This accomplished angler has received many honors throughout his career. Wallace fished the BASS Masters Classic in 1971 and 1973. He is a charter member of B.A.S.S. and the Virgil Ward Championship Fishing Club. He received the Distinguished Angler Award from Sports Afield in 1968 and in 2000 was inducted into the National Fresh Water Fishing Hall of Fame.

Ed Garcia and Charlie Marshall with 204 lbs. caught over a seven day period in April, 1970 near Campbell Point

A serious 1970's bass angler. Note stick steering, bait casters and tackle assortment.

A typical stringer of bass, mid-seventies, Eagle Rock

Chapter 8
The 80's

The trends that developed during the two previous decades continued on Table Rock during the 1980's. Interest in the lake and angling pressure saw steady growth. Advances in fishing techniques, tackle and equipment made the sport increasingly complex.

Lake levels varied quite a bit on Table Rock during the 80's. In 1980 the lake never rose to normal pool and was as low as 896. The reservoir finally reached normal pool by the end of 1981 and then crested about 12 feet high in December of 1982. The following two years, it fluctuated around normal pool, but peaked in January 1985 at over 929 feet. The rest of the decade saw variations of plus or minus about 10 feet.

Typically, Table Rock rises in the spring and then tapers off through the summer with occasional rises in the fall or winter. Lake levels are primarily influenced by rainfall in the watershed, but are also affected by power generation needs and conditions on the other White River impoundments- Beaver, Taneycomo and Bull Shoals. Table Rock is also somewhat restricted by the narrow margin of fluctuation allowed in little Taneycomo. The total volume of water in Table Rock Reservoir, 3,462,000 acre-feet, totally replaces itself about every one to two years.

Lake levels attract lots of interest from those living on or near the lake and from fishermen and vacationers. Constant fluctuations make dock tending more difficult and necessary. All docks on Table Rock are floating docks. Most are cabled to the shore and underwater anchors. Some use fixed stand-offs attached directly to the shoreline.

High water levels can make accesses unuseable and flood low

lying campgrounds. Low levels can make boat ramps inaccessible and expose underwater hazards. Fishermen would prefer to see levels raised in early spring and maintained at least until mid-summer. Higher water levels create good spawning habitat. Maintaining higher water helps protect fish fry and improves recruitment. The worst case scenario is high levels during the spawn which then drop quickly and dramatically. Lowering the water 5-10 feet during the spawn can be devastating to fish reproduction.

The Corps of Engineers' original mandate was to provide flood control, power generation and recreation. They also must consider agricultural and navigation needs far downstream of Table Rock. Over the years, this organization has begun to consider fisheries and wildlife populations as part of its responsibility. The amount of water held in a reservoir and the amount released through the dam are partially dependent on wildlife considerations. Despite man's attempts however, water levels in Table Rock are mostly dependent on rainfall and climatic conditions.

There were no major changes to fishing regulations during the 80's. The length and creel limits on black bass remained in place. The daily limit on crappie would be changed to 15 with a 10 inch minimum length. Bass tournaments probably had the largest effect on Table Rock fishing. Major improvements in bass boats, catch-and- release and aerated livewells all owe their widespread acceptance to tournament fishing. Although some criticism of tournament fishing was voiced, there was no scientific evidence that tournaments harmed the fishery. To the contrary, the conservation efforts supported by competitive fishing helped protect bass.

The most significant trend in fishing in this decade was improvements in fishing equipment. Rods and reels saw major advances. New models of baitcasting reels came to the market every year. Although round reels like the Ambassador remained very popular, new low profile models from manufacturers like Shimano and Daiwa were seeing more use. Zebco introduced their Quantum line in 1982. Daiwa and Penn developed reels with magnets for backlash control. Advances in gearing, level wind, braking systems and drag made baitcasters more effective tools. Spinning gear was also used widely on Table Rock, particularly as more subtle angling methods developed during the 80's.

A wide assortment of rod materials and styles became available. The use of graphite in rod construction improved their strength and sensitivity. Graphite rods became the tool of choice for most serious anglers. Fiberglass was still popular. The greater flexibility of fiberglass rods was sometimes preferred for crankbaits and topwaters since it provided a slight delay in hook sets. On the other hand, the hook setting feel and strength of graphite was often highly desirable-particularly for worm fishing.

Fishing rods were developed with strong butts and flexible tips. Cushioned handles with the rod blank extended through the grip provided comfort and feel. Pistol grips were common, but longer trigger grips were becoming popular. Seven to eight foot collapsible flipping sticks provided the length and power needed for this close-in technique. Special rods could be purchased for any type of fishing. There were spinnerbait rods, crankbait rods, worm rods and spooning rods. Each fish had its special tackle with "sticks" designed for bass, crappie, walleye, panfish, catfish and spoonbill.

Eyelets made of stainless steel, aluminum oxide or ceramic provided smooth casting and resistance to line abrasion. Boron rods were introduced in the 80's, but never became very popular- probably due to their high price and minimal improvement over graphite.

Many anglers now carried numerous rod and reel outfits in their boats. They often had five or six pre-rigged set-ups with different baits out on the casting deck ready for any situation.

Using medium weight spinning outfits with 6-8 lb. test line, anglers became increasingly adept at using lighter baits- particularly soft plastics. Especially toward the lower end of Table Rock from Campbell Point to the dam, lighter tackle and lures were effective in hooking all three sub-species of black bass. The soft plastic bait market exploded in the 1980's. All types, sizes, colors and styles of worms, grubs, lizards and trailers were developed and used.

Tube baits like the Gitzit saw extensive use on Table Rock. Popularized by fishermen like Guido Hibdon of Lake of the Ozarks, the tube bait was well suited to highland type reservoirs. Charlie Campbell helped introduce the Gitzit to Table Rock after seeing it used effectively on Lake Mead. Whether used around docks, standing timber, flooded vegetation or in sight fishing, skipping tube baits was an effective method.

Plastic worms got smaller and larger. Smaller versions of this classic bait were used in new so-called finesse techniques. Originated in the western United States on clear impoundments with minimal cover, finesse fishing was found to work on Table Rock. Heavy angling pressure, relatively clear water and diminishing cover were affecting the Rock's fish populations. Anglers responded by developing approaches that worked better on pressured, spooky fish. Longer casts with lighter tackle and smaller baits were sometimes required to entice these fish.

The wider assortment of soft plastics brought about many new designs and sizes of hooks. Offset shanks and wider throats provided applications for the numerous types of plastic baits used. The use of plastic beads and rattles became common. Beads were used between the hook and weight to protect the knot as well as to provide an attracting sound. Noise making rattles could be directly threaded on the line or inserted into soft plastics. Anglers were taking advantage of the technology to appeal to all the senses of gamefish.

However, "bubba baits" did not disappear. Large plastic worms up to 12 inches were used to take many lunker-sized bass. Other large baits like big spinnerbaits, topwaters and magnum crankbaits also worked well in the right patterns.

Crankbaits saw extensive development and use during the decade of the 80's. Short, wide-wobbling plugs like the Bomber Model A, Cotton Cordell Big-O, Rapala Shad Rap and Storm Wiggle Wart were effective throughout the year and under varying conditions. Crankbaits running to depths of ten to thirty feet worked well on the deep water of Table Rock. Super shallow models were used in special situations like surfacing fish and on shallow flats in the fall. The stickbait continued its reputation as a big fish lure, particularly during the pre-spawn period. As early as January, bass anglers would begin throwing suspending jerkbaits across open flats and around cedar groves.

The famous jig-and-pig retained its celebrity on Table Rock. Improvements in head styles and skirt materials, the addition of rattles and a variety of sizes and colors made this bait suitable for a wide range of conditions.

The 80's also saw extensive use of liquid scents. Research has shown that fish are attracted by scents and will hold a scented bait longer. Scents also help mask undesirable odors. For years, some anglers have applied various concoctions like fish oil, anise oil or even tobacco juice to their offerings. Dr. Loren Hill did considerable research showing the effectiveness of scents. The Berkley Co. developed several lines of baits with attractants already added. Liquid fish attractants became another tool anglers were using to increase their success.

Spinnerbaits, buzzbaits and various topwater selections continued to be used widely during the 80's. Despite the popularity and fishing pressure experienced by Table Rock Lake, this reservoir retained a reputation as an excellent fishery, particularly for bass.

Although night fishing had always been a good method on Table Rock, as fishing pressure increased, it became a more accepted way to improve angling success. The advantages to fishing after dark include fewer anglers, better stealth, possibly increased fish activity and at least in the summer, cooler temperatures. Table Rock was particularly well-suited for night fishing. Its relatively clear water means that fish are less spooky after sunset. Table Rock's depth and general lack of standing timber, at least in the main channel, make it fairly easy to navigate at night.

This area has a reputation for night fishing that goes back to the days when fishermen gigged fish from johnboats by the light of burning pine knots. By the 1980's, fishing after dark became a common practice for both local and visiting anglers. Some bass clubs even began having tournaments at night.

Even though any lure can be used at night, the most popular on Table Rock became the plastic worm, the jig-and-pig and the spinnerbait. Used in dark colors and fished slowly on rocky banks and around standing timber, these baits developed a reputation for catching big bass. Topwaters can also catch fish during this time of day, but are often hard to use effectively.

Two equipment options were developed during this period to make night fishing easier. The use of fluorescent line and black lights enabled after-hour anglers to see their line much better. This improved casting accuracy, bait presentation, line watching, hook set and the ability to play a fish properly. Without this type of gear, night fishing for bass was more difficult. Particularly from the spawn through September, night fishing became a frequently used method for successful angling on Table Rock.

1980's saw increased fishing during the winter months. Table Rock has always been fishable throughout the year. Several factors make it attractive as a year-round fishery. Located in southern Missouri, Table Rock experiences fairly mild winter weather. The lake never freezes over in the main channel, although ice does appear on the upper ends and in the coves for short periods.

The increase in tournament fishing created a breed of serious anglers looking for fishing opportunities in all seasons. Many of the growing number of people moving to and retiring to Table Rock liked to fish and wanted to fish as much as possible.

Winter techniques are generally employed December through February on the lake. After the fall feeding spree, deeper methods become the norm. Fishing ledges, channel edges and other deep structure with spoons or jigs can produce good catches of black bass. During the January thaw or periodic warm spells, fish will often move very shallow, particularly on rocky south-facing banks. These fish will take spinnerbaits, crankbaits and jig-and-pig, if fished slowly. Leadhead jigs dressed with small grubs or tubes will work on bass relating to structure and underwater trees during the colder months.

Starting in late January or early February as the surface temperatures move into the mid-40's, bass will begin to migrate toward staging areas. This is a hot time of year for jerkbaits on Table Rock. Flat-sided crankbaits and jigs will also take these staging fish. Late winter often produces some of the biggest bass on the reservoir.

The snowstorm phenomena can often produce some amazing results on this lake. Several anglers report excellent catches of largemouth, spotted and smallmouth bass on Table Rock during a blizzard. Late winter tournament results have verified these reports.

With the right clothing and gear, many Table Rock fishermen have found the lake enjoyable and productive in the winter months. Jim Patterson has fished the upper White area of Table Rock since

1966. He remembers winter fishing on the lake out of a Richline aluminum boat. To keep warm, he used a catalytic heater.

Crappie fishing saw a brief rise in success from 1979 through 1982 due to successful spawns in 1977 and 1979. Live minnows were the preferred method for crappies, but small jigs and spinners were being used more on this pressured species. In 1984, the daily limit of crappie on Table Rock was increased from 10 to 15, mostly to coincide with the limit on other Missouri impoundments and the 10" length limit was imposed lake-wide. Crappie fishing declined again in 1983 and remained just fair the rest of this decade. From 1983 through 1988, creel clerks found no anglers with a legal limit of 15 crappie. Despite decent conditions for crappie, particularly on the James River, this species was not able to maintain large numbers. This may have been due to the highly variable recruitment of year classes, fluctuations in water level and possibly loss of cover.[29]

Bill Anderson, Fisheries Biologist for the Department of Conservation, performed electrofishing for crappie in the James and Long Creek from 1987-1989. Big Creek was sampled in '87 and '88 and the Kings River was electrofished in 1988-89. The fish captured were almost exclusively white crappie. The only area yielding any significant black crappie was Big Creek.

Numbers for crappie varied considerably depending on the area and year. The Kings showed the best numbers during this period with over 50 fish per hour captured. The James had good numbers in 1987-8, but dropped dramatically in 1989. Long Creek and Big Creek had poor results for crappie. This study indicates crappie prefer the more fertile waters of areas like the Kings and James.[30]

Dock owners and resorts often developed their own crappie habitats. Sinking or hanging Christmas trees, cedar trees or brush under and around docks created good crappie cover. Although these beds did not always hold large numbers of fish, they often would yield a few nice-sized crappie. Gene Martin owner of Lunker Landing Resort in the 80's chummed his dock by suspending perforated cans of sauerkraut beneath his dock. He says this method worked well in attracting crappie and bass.

Novinger's study of the 15 inch length limit on bass showed

excellent bass fishing in the James River in the early 1980's.[31] Electrofishing in the James from 1973-1979 yielded an average of 122 largemouth bass per hour. The average from 1980-1983 was 224. Spotted bass saw similar increases. Bass fishing effort and success in Long Creek during the early 80's stayed about the same compared to the 70's. Angling effort was about four times greater in the James than in Long Creek. The total catch of largemouth and spotted bass was about ten times greater in the James than Long Creek.

The James River was obviously not only a popular area to fish, but also a very good area to fish. Credit for this is usually attributed to the rich, nutrient-laden waters of the James. As hard as it may be to accept, one source of these nutrients was point source pollution from Springfield and other towns and cities in the James River watershed. The dark eutrophic water of this stream created a rich food chain supporting an excellent fishery. The cleaner, clearer water of the main White, Long Creek and Indian Creeks was attractive, but did not support the fish populations that the richer James and Kings Rivers did. The Missouri Department of Conservation performed electrofishing studies on Table Rock from 1984 through 1989. Bill Anderson carried out this work during the black bass spawn on Big Creek from '84-'88, James River and Long Creek 1984-1989 and Kings River in 1988 and 1989.[32]

Catch rates for largemouth were the best on the James averaging 193 and the Kings 182 fish per hour. Big Creek and Long Creek had average rates for the period sampled of 135 and 126 respectively. Spotted bass numbers were much lower in all areas compared to largemouth, averaging about 28 fish per hour. The number of keeper- sized bass over 15" electrofished generally declined during this period.

Paddlefish stocking in the James River during the seventies began to pay off in the eighties. Nearly 83,000 paddlefish fingerlings were stocked in the James from 1972-1977. Mature paddlefish had probably spread throughout Table Rock, but the James remained the area that this species and paddlefish anglers preferred. Regulations permitted the harvest of paddlefish March 15 to May 15 and October 1 to December 31. In 1979 the spring season was shortened to March 15 to April 30. In 1987, a 24" length limit was imposed on spoonbills harvested.

The spoonbill is a filter feeder and is rarely caught by bait or lures. Snagging is the method used to harvest these large fish. In the spring, spoonbill move up tributaries to spawn on gravel bars. They seem to prefer high water and some current for spawning. Snagging is most successful during this period. Using heavy rods and reels with heavy line, one ounce sinkers and large treble hooks, snaggers drift or troll with the current or cast from the bank. Typically, a sweeping motion of the rod is used to keep the treble hooks moving through the water. When a hookup is made, the big fish are reeled in on the heavy equipment. This is exciting fishing and requires lots of upper body strength and stamina.

The James River provided a good habitat for paddlefish growth. The first year paddlefish reached snagging size on Table Rock was 1982. In this year, 200-300 fish were taken in the 30-40 lb. range. In 1983, as many as 2000 spoonbill were estimated in the harvest. A lower take was estimated in 1984, but the average size was 40 lbs.. Paddlefish spawning was documented in the James and in 1983 under high water conditions, they were snagged as far as 50 miles up the James.[33] Paddlefish snagging remained popular from 1985 through 1989 with over 2500 snaggers in each year. The catch rates were fair averaging over 700 keepers a year for the five year period. Average weights were well over 40 lbs.

Missouri's paddlefish program was so successful, the state sent 330,000 fry to the USSR during the 70's. Stocking of spoonbill fingerlings (8-19") continued with over 80,000 introduced into Table Rock between 1984 and 1990. Through hard work and study, the Department of Conservation had created a new, excellent paddlefish fishery in Table Rock Lake.

In 1985, 30,900 walleye fingerlings were stocked in Table Rock. These fish were 1-2 inches long and came from Merritt Reservoir in Nebraska. From 1981-3, 22 million walleye fry were also stocked. These fish helped establish a population which would eventually provide an alternative fishery in the reservoir.

Angler effort (the number of hours fished in a given area) in the James was very high in the early 80's. Surveys show angler effort stayed above 75 hours per acre through 1986. The number of fishing hours dropped off significantly in 1987 and averaged about 45 hours per acre through 1990. The reason for this decline is not known, but may be due to the heavy fishing pressure in this arm encouraging fishermen to seek other areas. In Long Creek, angler effort remained fairly stable around 30 hours/acre during this decade, peaking in 1989 at 35.7 hours/acre.[34]

The Department of Conservation performed creel surveys on the James River and Long Creek arms of Table Rock from March to November in 1986 through 1990. The practice was discontinued after 1990. Although useful, creel surveys had become too labor intensive and costly to support.

In the James, about 50% of the anglers surveyed were bass fishing. The numbers fishing for crappie and catfish were 15% and 10% respectively. In Long Creek, bass fishing accounted for an average of about 70% of the effort. Crappie fishermen made up only about 10% of the total hours.

Black bass catch rates were good in the James averaging around one fish per two hours fished. Long Creek bass anglers caught about one fish every three hours. As seems to be inherent to Table Rock, crappie catch rates varied considerably year to year. The James showed good crappie fishing in 1986, 1987 and 1990. Despite little effort for crappie, Long Creek produced good catch rates in 1986-1988, but poor results in '89 and '90. White bass fishing was very good in the James from 1986-1989, but almost non-existent in 1990. In Long Creek, 1986 and 1987 saw good results for white bass despite little angler effort. The remainder of the decade apparently attracted very little interest in white bass. The James produced good catches of channel cat throughout the survey period. The few anglers who did catch catfish in Long Creek saw only limited success, primarily for channel cat.[35]

Table Rock was a favored site for tournaments during the 1980's. Most of these competitions were for bass anglers, but there was an occasional crappie tournament. The Missouri State Water Patrol tracks fishing tournaments by requiring a permit for each event. Although there were certainly some smaller club tourneys that did not obtain permits, the Water Patrol's figures give a good indication of the number and size of these events.

Between 1980 and 1989 there were an average of 237 fishing tournaments a year on Table Rock. The number varied from year to year with a low of 166 in 1981 and a high of 292 in 1988. More interesting is the size of these events. The 224 outings in 1980 involved 4,000 boats. The number of craft increased almost every year peaking in 1986 with over 10,000 boats fishing in 253 tournaments. Participation remained high through the end of this decade.

The popularity of fishing tournaments continued to parallel the development of the bass boat. Fishing boats got longer, more powerful and more sophisticated in the 80's.

To get his fish to the weigh-in in good shape, a tournament angler needed a good livewell. Most 1980's boats came equipped with large, divided livewells with fresh water pumps, recirculation and aeration. Additives like Catch and Release became popular to help insure the survival of livewelled fish. Trolling motors increased their amount of thrust and added break-away clutches to handle the increased weight and speed of bass boats.

Many anglers had become very adept at reading flasher graphs. With lots of practice, a good flasher reader could distinguish fish, schools of shad and trees and gauge bottom composition. Unfortunately, the average fisherman wasn't this skilled at reading flashers and relied on them primarily for depth readings. Paper graphs were capable of supplying information in a more readable format. However, they tended to be expensive and somewhat difficult to maintain.

The introduction of the LCG (Liquid Crystal Graph) in the eighties made reading sonar blips easier and more informative. These units became standard on almost all bass boats sold in the 80's. Many boaters used an LCG at the bow when fishing and a flasher at the console when driving.

There's a long standing discussion over the best place to mount a sonar unit's transducer. Transom mounts are always working, but only show the water you've already passed. Trolling motor bow mounts give excellent data directly below while fishing, but nothing while running. Through-hull mounted transducers provide a compromise, but are difficult to replace. Most anglers developed a preference for their individual style or mounted two or more units. Other fishing aids developed during the decade of the 80's include the Color-C-Lector, pH meters, oxygen level sensors and electronic thermometers. Although based on scientific evidence, with the exception of thermometers, these tools never attained ongoing acceptance.

Angling safety was improved due to the influence of fishing tournaments. Restrictions on maximum horsepower, the required use of life jackets and kill switches all came about largely through the influence of organized competitive angling. Shotgun take-offs had been the norm during the seventies. Because of numerous accidents, this exciting, but dangerous practice was replaced with the sequential, one boat at a time take-offs during the 80's.

Bass fishing had become a skilled, professional sport. Table Rock Lake can be proud that many fine fishermen developed their skills here. Bass pros like Charlie Campbell, Stacey King, Rick Clunn and Larry Nixon fished Table Rock regularly. This White River impoundment was also featured on many regional television and radio fishing shows. Anglers like Virgil Ward and Harold Ensley often fished Table Rock and featured these trips on their programs.

The basic bass boat was fully developed by this decade. Fiberglass models were by far the norm, but good quality aluminum boats were often used. Most resorts supplied or rented smaller aluminum fishing boats. Pontoon boats were also popular, but were better suited to still fishing for crappie, bluegill or catfish.

Bass boats manufactured by companies like Ranger, Champion, Bass Cat and Skeeter were well suited to fishing Table Rock. These fishing machines, 16 to 20 feet in length and powered by 115-175 hp. 2-stroke motors could get to any spot on Table Rock's waters. With high performance V6 outboards, these boats could reach speeds up to 80 mph getting anglers to their fishing holes quickly. Trolling motors with up to 50 lbs. of thrust could handle a full day of fishing the bluffs, flats, coves, channels, points and humps of Table Rock, even in a heavy wind.

Special equipment and gear developed during the 80's to handle the high speeds of boats. Almost all boats had console mounted steering. Many had windshields. Gas tanks were bigger and most motors used oil injection. Instrument panels included engine temperature, water pressure, oil pressure and warning lights and alarms. Most boaters chose to have instrument panel depth finders or at least sonar units mounted at the console for running. A second unit was usually mounted at the bow for use when fishing. Trim and tilt controls were necessary for proper performance on these rigs. Special prop designs made by companies like Predator allowed for quick hole shots and blistering high-end speeds. Hull designs had developed to the point where many modern boats were running on only about two feet of pad at the stern when cruising. To aid stability, bass boats were widened to beams of 80 inches and greater on the longer models. V-hull designs originated by companies like Allison Craft and Hydra Sports also helped improve performance and stability. Bright colored metal flake gel coats, quality marine carpet and heavy duty upholstery made these boats attractive and comfortable.

Due to the influence of tournaments and the speeds being attained, most anglers were now using life jackets and kill switches when running. Raised, carpeted decks provided good fishing platforms. Large, lockable storage, long rod boxes, insulated coolers, roomy livewells and removable, adjustable fishing chairs were standard on most craft. The butt seat saw common use, particularly at the bow. Many anglers preferred to stand when fishing. Standing allows freer casting, better vision, quicker reactions and better leverage.

Boat trailers had to increase in size to handle the larger bass boats. Most fishing rigs were bought as a package with the boat, motor and trailer matched by the retailer. Trailers required heavier suspensions and larger wheels. Some even had surge braking systems.

To handle heavy, long, expensive boats, the towing vehicle became a serious consideration for many fishermen. The pickup truck was the most popular, but vans and station wagons also served well. Boaters had to make sure they had good quality hitches and wiring harnesses on their towing vehicles. The increase in cost and sophistication of boats encouraged more Table Rock boat owners to use lifts in their dock slips. The proliferation of on-shore storage facilities for boats began in the 80's as more locals and visitors required secure storage for their craft.

High performance fishing boats had an effect on fishing clothing. Exposure at the speeds these boats were capable of, particularly in cold weather, required special garments. Two-piece rain suits with hoods and elastic cuffs kept the rain and wind at bay. Products like Gore-Tex and Thinsulate, originally developed primarily for hunting, were used in fishing apparel. In cold weather, face masks and even racing helmets were used to protect anglers.

Increasingly in this decade, fishermen were demanding special clothing. Shirts, pants, jackets, shoes and gloves were all being developed with fishing comfort and utility in mind. Insulated brrr suits were necessary for fishing on Table Rock during the winter. This lake can be fished effectively year-round, but proper attire is required for the four distinct seasons of the Ozarks.

Most serious fishermen used sunglasses. Widespread use of polarized glasses had an important effect on fishing. Polarized sunglasses allow the wearer to see more clearly and deeper into the water. This is a definitive advantage for seeing fish and objects in the lake. Sight fishing during the spawning season is much easier with polarized glasses. They also allow an angler to see underwater objects farther away and make longer, accurate casts- a distinct benefit in clear water conditions.

As professional fishing became more sophisticated, many tournament competitors sought sponsorship. These relationships encouraged communication between anglers and fishing equipment manufacturers. More and more, fishing items of all types were designed with input from fishermen. This development not only improved equipment, but it increased the economic impact of fishing. When you consider the cost of the boat, trailer, towing vehicle, tackle and equipment, an angler could easily spend thousands of dollars. Added to the expense of accommodations, meals, gasoline and licenses, fishing became an economic boon to the Table Rock area. In 1980, Table Rock was ranked 6th as the most visited Corps project in the country with an estimated 6 million visitor days.

Fishing not only pumps thousands of dollars into the Table Rock Lake area, it is a largely self-supporting sport. Since 1950, the Sport Fish Restoration Act (Dingell-Johnson Act) has supported fisheries and boating through a 10% excise tax on fishing tackle. These monies are redistributed through state sponsored fishery projects. Since its inception, this program has infused over $3.6 billion into fishing and boating.

In 1984, the Wallop-Breaux amendment supplemented the Sports Fish and Restoration Act by including excise taxes on additional fishing equipment, a 3% tax on trolling motors and depth finders, import duties on fishing tackle and pleasure boats and a portion of motorboat fuel taxes. Wallop-Breaux increased the funds significantly for state programs. In 1999, over $212 million was generated.

These programs and others like Missouri's 1/8% Conservation sales tax are examples of how anglers underwrite their own avocation. The numbers of anglers and their economic clout made it possible for fishermen to have political influence. Particularly through B.A.S.S., B.A.S.S. Federation clubs and groups like the Missouri Bass Club Association, anglers could promote legislation and projects favorable to fishing.

Bill Anderson has worked as the Missouri Department of Conservation's Fisheries Biologist on Table Rock since the mid-80's. He has developed an excellent understanding of the lake and its fisheries. Bill supervises the creel surveys, netting, electrofishing, fish stocking and habitat development projects on Table Rock. He has been instrumental in building the spoonbill and walleye populations and protecting the bass and crappie fisheries.

Bill began fishing this lake in the early 60's. His personal experience and association with many of Table Rock's best anglers have led him to develop keen angling skills. He has fished all over Table Rock using both shallow and deep techniques. One of his biggest fish is a 7lb.9oz. largemouth taken near Indian Point in 1965 on a Hellbender.

Anderson has supported lowering the length limit on Kentuckies to 12" for several years. He would like to see lake levels maintained throughout the spawn and periodic drawdowns to encourage shoreline vegetation. Bill supports habitat development through planting of Christmas and cedar trees, but feels this primarily tends to concentrate fish and does not necessarily increase populations.

Bill Beck of Kimberling City has fished this lake since the 60's. His family owned Schooner Creek Resort from 1966 to 1997. Bill has worked as a fishing guide on Table Rock since the early 70's. In the 60's, Bill remembers using an Ambassador reel on a fiberglass rod and also spinning outfits with blue Trilene monofilament. Some of his favorite lures were plastic worms, the Zara Spook, Rebel Super R, Brown Bomber and Dixie Jet Flutter Spoon. The Dixie Jet was a ¾ oz. spoon in chrome or gold cast around tree tops in 20-25 ft. of water. Bill also caught crappie and bass on crappie jigs in white or grey.

In the early days on Table Rock, there were many fishing guides working on the lake. Beck says there were ten full-time guides working out of Baxter in the 60's. There were two men on the dock at night selling live bait and assisting night fishermen. In the 70's, guides like Bill Beck began fishing open water more. Using the "Green Box" flasher and their own knowledge of the lake's structure, they used small plastic worms and weedless jigs on spotted bass and largemouth bass. During the winter, many locals and guides fished spoons up to 75 feet deep.

In the 80's, Bill began developing finesse tactics. He fished with Bobby Garland in a U.S. Bass tournament in 1983. Bobby won the tournament using a "western style" gitzit with a spider jig attached. He dropped the bait on an exposed hook ⅜ oz. jig in about 35 ft. of water. This technique not only influenced Bill, it helped begin the widespread use of finesse tactics on Table Rock.

Beck started using the Carolina- rig with Zoom French fries and Fish Doctors. In the 90's, he employed split-shotting effectively. Using spinning tackle with 8# test line in water up to about 25 feet, this technique was deadly on bass, particularly March through October. Beck usually employs soft plastic baits on a small worm hook with a #4 round split-shot attached 18" up the line. He prefers green pumpkin colors. More recently, Bill has used drop-shotting for suspended fish. During tough summer conditions, Beck will use live nightcrawlers to help his guiding customers catch some fish.

Bill Beck has seen some changes in the resort business over the years. In the early years, most vacationers did not own a boat. Although some did bring a motor, many relied on the resort to supply a boat. Guides were hired by many lake visitors. Although Table Rock resorts have always had lots of family vacationers, the growth of bass tournaments has added many new customers. Over the years, more and more people began bringing their own boats to the lake.

Originally, most fish caught were kept, cleaned and eaten. As catch-and-release has gained wider acceptance, most fish are now set free. Out of about 150 guide trips in 2002, Bill said he cleaned fish only five times. Fishing has gotten tougher over the years requiring better equipment and skills from Table Rock anglers. Guides have had to adapt by using more finesse techniques and even live bait.

The number of resorts on Table Rock has not increased in the last few years. Many of the new resorts are condominium developments without the same amenities provided by the traditional resorts. Nevertheless, the resort business remains strong with second and third generations returning to the same locations for Table Rock vacations.

Bill Beck is cautiously optimistic about the future of fishing on this lake. He is pleased with the strong Kentucky population and the increase in the number of smallmouth seen. He hopes recent signs of bigger largemouth are an indication this sub-species is rebounding.

One of Bill's best fishing days came in 1974 when he was guiding as a 17 year old. It was a bluebird day in October. Fishing for an hour and a half on a roadbed using a flutter spoon, he had ten Kentuckies weighing 46 pounds near the mouth of the James. He outfished all the other guides that day and raised his status considerably.

A spoonbill taken from the Roaring River arm, mid-80's

Charlie Campbell. Note Woodwalker bait.

Chapter 9
The 90's

As Table Rock Lake moved into its fourth decade, fishing remained good. The programs, regulations and conservation practices of the 70's and 80's had resulted in one of the best black bass fisheries in the nation. Stable populations of paddlefish and walleye presented additional opportunities for anglers. Although crappie continued to suffer from widely varying recruitment, fishermen who knew when and how to fish for this species could do well. In general, crappie numbers were not great, but the size quality was good.

Anglers on "the Rock" continued to develop their skills. Many new techniques, patterns and baits were developed to catch fish. Equipment kept increasing in complexity and technology. Fishing pressure increased, especially for bass. In a survey done from 1988-1994, Table Rock ranked first for the most recreational visitors to Missouri Corps lakes averaging 30-40 million visitors a year. In 1991, another study found Table Rock to be the most heavily fished lake in the state.[36]

As the nineties dawned on Table Rock, water quality concerns became more common. Despite the overall high water quality of the lake, rapid development throughout the watershed was putting certain areas of Table Rock at risk. Local grassroots organizations, resort owners, cities, chambers of commerce, the Department of Conservation and the Department of Natural Resources began paying more attention to the reservoir's water and its wildlife. It was becoming apparent that the quality of the resource was being threatened by those who desired to live near it and enjoy its benefits.

Table Rock was also beginning to show its age. The process of eutrophication occurs in all lakes over time. Typically, the amount of nutrients in a body of water increases with time. As nutrients such as nitrogen and phosphorus flow into a lake from the watershed, the level of eutrophication rises. These nutrients provide the basis for the food chain and determine to a large extent the biomass the lake will support. Phosphorus and nitrogen provide food for algae which in turn supports aquatic insects. Insects are fed upon by small fishes which are then eaten by larger fish. Ultimately, man becomes the final predator. A strong nutrient base is therefore beneficial for a fishery. However, when nutrient levels rise too high or are out of balance, the lake's fishing will decline.

Oligotrophic waters are very clear and have low algae production. These are great conditions for swimming, skiing and diving, but provide a limited resource for fish populations. Mesotrophic describes a lake with moderate productivity. The water will have some color to it. A larger population of fish and wildlife can be supported. Eutrophic lakes have good algae production. Eutrophic waters will usually support very good fisheries, but the decreased water clarity may impair swimming and diving. When a body of water contains too many nutrients, it becomes hypereutrophic. The water will be very dark with lots of algae growth. Reduced oxygen levels lead to decreased ability to support fish.

Since Table Rock is a large lake with a large watershed, the eutrophication levels vary considerably throughout the reservoir. Other factors like rainfall and changes in land usage also affect the productivity of different areas of the lake. Over the years, Table Rock has undergone many changes in its water quality. The James River has always been one of the most nutrient rich arms of the lake (see pp.11 and 55). It has also always been one of the best fishing areas. The Kings River has basically paralleled the James' condition, although it has been less affected by urban effluent.

Most of the White River section has generally had clear water and average nutrient loads. One exception is the upper White above Eagle Rock. Before Beaver Dam was completed, this area contained somewhat darker, richer water. After 1964, the water became clearer and colder. The lower lake area has to this day maintained an oligotrophic state. Long Creek has generally been a clear arm. It is more susceptible to inflows due to its size and watershed. Fish population studies almost always show lower numbers of fish in Long Creek compared to the James. Arms like Big and Little Indian Creek with fairly undeveloped watersheds generally have clear water.

As Table Rock aged, the amount of visible cover declined. There are still lots of standing trees along some of the bluff banks and in many coves, but their density decreases every year. For the first few years, Table Rock contained huge amounts of flooded trees and brush. These conditions are largely responsible for the exceptional bass and crappie fishing in the early years. Not only did the cover provide excellent living conditions for fish, it made fishing easy. As water levels varied in the reservoir, the steep shorelines of Table Rock lost their soil and their ability to sustain vegetation. Much cover still existed, but it was not visible.

Over time, changes in water quality and lake conditions have affected the fish populations. Starting in the 80's, more spotted bass and smallmouth bass were showing up in Table Rock. These subspecies seem to prefer the deep, clear arms with rocky cover. During this period, reports of a cross between smallmouth and spotted bass arose. Although this hybrid had probably existed in the White River watershed for years, it was only recently positively identified. The "meanmouth" generally has the markings of a Kentucky and the coloring of a smallie, but variations exist. Part of the hybrid's mystery is their difficult identification. Often they can only be accurately identified by biological testing. Meanmouth have a reputation for aggressive strikes and pole-bending runs.

Table Rock anglers adapted well to changing conditions on the lake. During the 90's, techniques which worked well for Kentucky and smallmouth bass were finely tuned. Fishermen began to fish deeper and with more finesse.

Lake levels were fairly stable during the 1990's on Table Rock, never dropping below 904. The highest level reached was 929 in May 1990.

The Missouri Department of Conservation temporarily discontinued most angler surveys in 1991. Starting in 1991, they based fish population studies primarily on electrofishing.[37] Angler surveys were conducted on the James and mid-White arms in 1995 through 1997. Electrofishing was performed annually at night during the spring on the James, Kings and Long Creek. The mid-White electrofishing began in 1995.

From 1991 through 1994, the James and Kings showed excellent populations of black bass with good growth rates. Long Creek had fewer bass, but had a sound population with good percentages of keepers. Kentuckies made up about 25% of the total bass counted in these studies. They may have been somewhat underreported due to their tendency to spawn deeper making them less susceptible to electrofishing.

Electrofishing results for 1995 through 1999 showed strong bass populations in the James and Kings and good numbers in Long Creek and the mid-White (between Campbell Point and the James). Spotted bass continued to make up a good portion of the black bass captured. In 1999, spots accounted for 16% of the bass in Kings River and 38% in Long Creek.

Due to their slower growth rate, Kentucky populations included large numbers of sub-legal fish. The Department of Conservation continued to recommend the length limit on spots be lowered to 12 inches. The Department's position on spotted bass was that reducing their legal limit would allow more average fishermen to keep some fish for consumption. Some guides also supported this measure to help their clients keep more fish. Others felt that reducing the limit would tend to overharvest this species. There was also a concern that some anglers would misidentify largemouth as Kentuckies. This recommendation has yet to be enacted.

The crappie population in the 90's was generally weak on Table Rock. Although their numbers were low, their growth rates were good with crappie reaching the legal 10" limit by age three. The James and Kings produced the best crappie fishing, while the clearer White and Long Creek areas yielded very low numbers.

Creel surveys[38] conducted 1995-1997 showed considerable angler effort in the James and moderate effort in the mid-White. Catch rates for black bass were good in both areas. In the James, about 75% of the fishing was for black bass. This number was over 90% in the White. The James produced similar catch rates for spotted and largemouth bass. In the mid-White, spotted bass actually out-numbered the largemouth caught. A few smallmouth were caught in the White, but very few were taken in the darker James. The percentage of legal fish released varied from 26% to over 50%.

Crappie fishing was still practiced fairly often in the James with good catch rates of legal fish. Almost all of these fish were white crappie. There was little effort for crappie in the main lake area. There was only sporadic effort for white bass in either arm. Some anglers fished for catfish in the James with reasonable success. The great majority of this species taken were channel catfish.

Although not fully reflected in creel surveys, white bass fishing is a popular pastime on Table Rock. The best time for white bass is in the spring starting around March 1st. These fish make spring runs up the major tributaries. The Kings has one of the best runs, but the James, Long Creek and the upper White also see numbers of white bass. White bass fishing also occurs in late summer and early fall when these fish chase large schools of shad in open water throughout the lake.

In the spring, the preferred method of catching whites is trolling the channels with medium depth crankbaits and in-line spinners. Later in the year, whites are caught by casting shallow crankbaits, spinners, spoons or topwaters into schools of feeding fish. Either method can produce large catches of nice-sized fish. Timing and location are critical to white bass fishing. They feed sporadically on and off throughout the day. When you're at the right place at the right time, you can really load up.

White bass on Table Rock have excellent growth rates. Whites typically attain 16" lengths by age four. White bass seldom live much past this age. Their annual recruitment varies considerably and whites seem to be largely dependent on the availability of their major food source- threadfin shad. Table Rock has excellent populations of threadfin which contribute to their good growth. There is a daily limit of 15 combined white bass and their hybrids and a limit of 4 over 18 inches.

Interest in paddlefish snagging declined considerably during the decade of the 90's. This decline is mostly attributed to a level III health advisory issued in 1990. The level of chlordane detected in paddlefish samples collected in 1988 and 1989 exceeded the action level of 300 ppb. There was also a perception of poor taste to Table Rock paddlefish.[39] Starting in 1990, paddlefish did not exceed the chlordane limit, but angler interest did not start to rebound until 1998. An article in Field & Stream by Joel Vance about Table Rock paddlefishing helped increase interest in this fishery. The fall snagging season was eliminated in 1990. In 1998 and 1999, the number of snaggers began to rise.

10,195 spoonbill fingerlings were stocked in 1998. In 1999, 3000 fingerlings were released into Table Rock. This lake was serving as the source for paddlefish broodstock. Each year, large paddlefish are captured in the James in gillnets. These fish supply the eggs and milt for raising spoonbill in Missouri's hatcheries.

Electrofishing for walleye in the upper Kings River started in 1998. Good numbers of large walleye were collected. These fish showed excellent growth rates reaching the 18" legal limit between their second and third year. Even more walleye were captured in 1999. The Table Rock walleye fishery was small, but well established. Each spring, these fish make a spawning run well up the Kings. Efforts to electrofish walleye up the James in 1999 were unsuccessful.

Walleye fishing received little attention on Table Rock until the late 90's. When people began catching walleye while fishing for other species, interest increased. Trolling large stickbaits on main lake gravel flats has produced some good walleye fishing on the White between Shell Knob and Eagle Rock. The best quality walleye come from the upper Kings in late winter as the fish move up to spawn. Drifting live minnow rigs is the best method for these fish. Based on electrofishing results and angler reports, the walleye fishery on Table Rock is capable of producing good quality fish for those with the skill and knowledge to catch "eyes". Walleye have a length limit of 18" and a daily limit of four on Table Rock.

Many water quality issues were raised on Table Rock during the 1990's. The lake's clear, clean water was under assault from several sources. Development and populations around the lake were increasing dramatically. The Branson "boom" accounted for much of this growth, but all areas around Table Rock experienced considerable population increases in this decade. From 1990 to 2000, the counties of Barry, Christian, Greene, Stone and Taney increased population by 27% or almost 85,000 people.

In addition to human sewage, there were increasing nutrient loads entering the lake from agricultural sources. Run-off from livestock operations and fertilizer applications contributed to non-point source pollution. The explosion of large scale poultry operations in Missouri and Arkansas added significantly to the nutrients in Table Rock's watershed. Run-off from landfills and construction sites contributed their share. The natural process of eutrophication was being accelerated on Table Rock.

Toxic chemicals like lead, mercury and chlordane, which came from a variety of sources, were a cause for concern. Chlordane content caused a health advisory on paddlefish in 1990 and a mercury health advisory was issued for consumption of largemouth bass over 12" for selected individuals in 2001.

The Lakes of Missouri Volunteer Program (LMVP) started testing water samples from Table Rock in 1992. This organization supported by the EPA, the Missouri DNR and the University of Missouri uses local volunteers to take water samples from various locations on lakes throughout Missouri. Samples are collected about every three weeks April through September. Secchi disk readings are also taken.

A Secchi disk is an 8" round disk painted in four alternating black and white quadrants. The disk is lowered on a rope into water until it disappears from view. The length of rope from the surface of the water to the disk is then measured. This measurement gives a good indication of water clarity. The Secchi disk was first used by Fr. Pietro Secchi, an advisor to the Vatican in 1865 to measure water clarity and depth in the Mediterranean Sea.

LMVP water samples are filtered and submitted for testing. The amount of nitrogen, phosphorus and chlorophyll are measured. These amounts are good indicators of the algae population in a given body of water. These measurements can be used to establish the trophic state of the water.

The LMVP started testing at two sites on Table Rock in 1992, one near Baxter and one on the James. By 2000, the number of sites had risen to 17 and included all areas and arms of the lake. Most of the areas tested yielded chlorophyll values indicating mesotrophic or eutrophic states. Two sites documented oligotrophic values. Of concern were the hypereutrophic readings from sampling at two

Trophic Assessment of sites on Table Rock Lake based on average chlorophyll values.

Site	1992	1993	1994	1995	1996	1997	1998	1999	2000	2001	2002
1		M	M	E	O	M	M	M	M	O	M
2		M	E	E	M	M	M	E	M	O	M
3	E	E	E	E	M	M	M	E	M	O	M
4.5				E	M	M	E	E	M	M	E
5	E	E		E	E	E	E		E	E	E
6.5					E	E	E	E	E	E	E
7					E	E	E	E	E	E	E
8		M	E	E	M	M	E	E	M	M	E
9			E	E	M	M	M	E	M	M	E
10			M	E	M	M	M	E	M	O	E
11				E	E	E	E				E
12				H	E	E	H	H	E	E	E
13				H	H	H	H	E	H	H	E
14								E	O	O	M
15								E	M	M	E
16									E	E	E
17									M	M	E
18									M	O	E

O = Oligotrophic
M = Mesotrophic
E = Eutrophic
H = Hypereutrophic

locations on the upper James. Although yearly averages on the upper Kings were eutrophic, occasional individual samples were hypereutrophic in nature. Secchi readings vary widely on Table Rock. The minimum reading in 2000 was 24" on the James. The clearest water was at the dam where Secchi depths up to 188" were measured.[40]

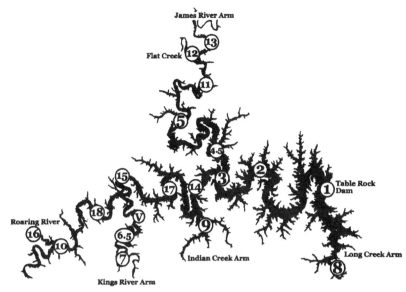

Location of Table Rock Lake   sample sites.

These data have not yet indicated any trends on Table Rock, but they do provide important baseline information which can be used to judge future developments on the lake. They also help locate potential problem areas. The Kings and James have always had some of the best fishing prospects on Table Rock. Their nutrient levels are largely responsible for this. However, the existence of hypereutrophic algae populations in these arms are cause for concern. Nutrient loads at these levels can lead to fish kills, as well as very unattractive water conditions.

As Table Rock has aged, there has been a general perception that the lake is decreasing in clarity. Many people who have enjoyed the lake for years relate how the water was much clearer in the past. A study of the data collected over the years tells a slightly different story.

Water clarity varies considerably based on various factors. Two of the major determinants on Table Rock are inorganic suspended solids and algae. Suspended solids enter the lake primarily through runoff from rain. Algae growth runs in cycles and is mostly based on the availability of nutrients like phosphorus and nitrogen. Other factors which can affect clarity are temperature and current.

In its early years, Table Rock's watershed consisted of large undeveloped forest areas, agricultural acreage and relatively small towns. This topography led to mostly clear water. When it rained, agricultural runoff dumped plenty of silt and nutrients into the lake. The lack of adequate sewage treatment from the existing towns also contributed heavy nutrient loads. These conditions accounted for the darker water in the James, Kings and the upper White before Beaver Dam.

With time, as the area developed, more human created inflows from sewage and construction would have contributed to reduced clarity. Improvements in agricultural practices reduced erosion in the watershed and should have slowed this trend somewhat. Recent awareness of water quality issues has prompted several projects which should help keep the water of Table Rock clean. Specifically, phosphorus removal by municipal sewage treatment plants should help significantly in reducing the nutrient load. By early 2003, Springfield and Branson plants had phosphorus removal on-line. Ozark, Nixa and Cassville were in various stages of installing upgraded treatment. Arkansas did not require phosphorus removal and Berryville had no plans to install this capability.

Secchi readings taken by trained personnel over the years on Table Rock show that water clarity has varied considerably. Some areas have almost always been dark while others are generally very clear. Readings change dramatically from year to year and even weekly, often due to climatic conditions.

In the early 1960's Secchi readings on the White near Indian Point were often over 15 feet. During the same period, readings in the James averaged only about three feet. In the early 70's, Long Creek had measurements around 10-11'. The James remained fairly dark with Secchi depths of 4-5'. The early 80's saw results similar to the 70's.[41]

In the early 90's there were signs of decreasing water clarity throughout the lake. In the mid-White near Kimberling City, summer readings averaged around ten feet. In Long Creek they were about eight feet and the James remained around three feet.

In 2001, the lake seemed to clear up dramatically. Near

Kimberling City, 14' depths were measured. Long Creek showed 13' and even the James had readings of 6-7'. Secchi tests done near the dam had a mean summer value of 20' with a maximum reading of nearly 26 feet. 2002 reflected the reverse. Although tests at Kimberling City were still around 15', Long Creek had darkened to an average of 6 to 7 feet and the James was back to about 4'.[42]

These data indicate that although Table Rock is probably not as clear on the average as it was forty years ago, it still has the potential for very clear water. Depending on human development, natural processes, weather and improvements in runoff and effluent control, Table Rock certainly has the potential to remain a clear water lake for years to come.

During the 1990's, Table Rock fishermen acquired many new techniques and baits. Traditional lures and patterns were still used, but many new ones were developed to meet the challenges of a changing fishery.

Baitcasting outfits remained the tackle of choice for almost all anglers. High quality baitcasting reels on graphite rods could be found on just about every casting deck on the lake. Many anglers also employed spinning tackle, particularly for the lighter finesse tactics gaining in popularity. Rods and reels were often very specialized with reel speed ratios, rod length and rod flexibility matched to particular techniques. Flipping generally decreased in popularity on Table Rock during the 90's.

Many new styles of line became available during this decade. Stronger, narrower monofilament enabled anglers to use lighter lines with more confidence. Some lines had less stretch and were more flexible. A variety of colors from clear to green to ultraviolet could be used for different conditions. New braided line touted for its superb strength, was briefly popular in the early nineties. It never gained widespread usage due to its lack of flexibility and poor spool characteristics.

One of the biggest developments in techniques during this decade was finesse tactics. Finesse has become a broad descriptive term, but it generally refers to techniques with lighter line, equipment and lures. Carolina-rigging became very popular on Table Rock in the

1990's. This approach is typically used in water depths of 0-20ft. A sliding weight is placed on the line above a swivel or snap. A bead is often placed between the weight and snap. A worm hook is tied to a short piece of line, usually 18-24", and this line is tied to the snap. A soft plastic bait is placed on the hook. The hook may be exposed or rigged weedless. Common baits are worms, lizards, creatures, grubs and tube baits. Typically, these are small lures, 4" or shorter. Sometimes floating baits are used to keep the offering off the bottom.

A Carolina-rig is cast out and slowly drug or trolled across the bottom. The weight bounces along creating noise and stirring up silt. The plastic bait swims along behind the weight presenting an attractive offering for fish.

This technique was found to work particularly well on the rocky shorelines of Table Rock. Even in areas with minimal cover, Carolina-rigs caught lots of bass during the 90's. This approach was particularly effective on the increasing population of Kentucky bass in the lake. A variation on the Carolina-rig is split-shotting. This technique employs lighter tackle and lighter line. In place of a sliding egg sinker, a split- shot is attached about 18" above a small worm hook.

Another finesse tactic used was light jigging. A small lead-head jig, with or without a small spinner, is dressed with a bait like a French fry, Zoom worm, razor worm, curly tailed grub or tube bait. This rig almost always employs an exposed hook. The bait is typi-cally fished as vertically as possible around standing trees or on structure like points, humps and channel bends. This rig can be fished at almost any depth, but is probably most effective at depths of 10 to 60 feet. Anglers like Ralph Lambert of Shell Knob have used this technique to catch large numbers of bass, often in one location. Ralph fishes this rig very subtly and sometimes even removes the hook barb.

In the late 90's, drop-shotting became popular on Table Rock. Drop-shotting is a variation on the Carolina-rig. The weight is attached at the line's terminal end and a hook is placed several inches above the weight. Small soft plastic baits are used as lures. This rig has the advantage of keeping the bait off the bottom better.

It also works well with live bait.

In their continuing search for new methods, Table Rock anglers began using the pitching technique. A variation of flipping, pitching is a casting method for accurate, quick placement of baits on average length casts. With the reel on free spool, the lure is held in one hand. The rod is held low and then lifted to propel the bait toward the target. This delivery works well with medium to heavy lures.

Other approaches like doodling and the use of do-nothing worms saw some use on the reservoir during this decade. These finesse techniques were effective on the pressured fish of Table Rock. Increasing populations of spotted and smallmouth bass were more susceptible to these fishing styles. Reduced visible cover on the lake also contributed to the success of these approaches. Finesse tactics have the advantage of working all year on Table Rock. Spring and fall generally call for shallower patterns. Summer's hot temperatures usually require deeper angling. In the winter, deep and slow are called for.

Many varieties of lures became available in the 90's on Table Rock. Soft plastic baits were very popular and came in many shapes, sizes and colors. Traditional plastic worms were still widely used and retained their renown as a big fish bait and also as a good night bait. Floating worms were used for shallow fish, especially in the spring. The general trend in plastic offerings was smaller. Simple designs in 3 to 4 inches were the convention.

Trailer baits countered the finesse trend with many getting larger and more complex. Plastic craws with many appendages were often the preferred trailer on jig-and-craw. Toward the end of this decade, creature baits became popular. These soft plastics had all kinds of legs, arms and wings, giving them good buoyancy and a large profile. They were used with traditional Texas-rigs and also Carolina- and drop- shot rigs.

Many soft plastics were manufactured with salt, scent or flavors impregnated in them. Gel scent additives which reduced the mess of some spray-ons became available. Granular attractants were marketed which could be placed in bags of soft plastics for adsorption of scent and flavor. After anglers began experimenting with inserting Alka Seltzer tablets into baits, the tackle industry developed similar products. When inserted into soft lures, these "fizz" tablets produced attractive bubbles and scent. Many soft plastic baits were developed with openings for the placement of scents or fizzers. To further improve the lure of these baits, some fishermen on Table Rock inserted small rattles into their soft plastics. Combination baits with hard plastic bodies and replaceable soft tails were introduced in the 90's. They do not appear to have gained much acceptance on Table Rock. Tube baits remained popular in a variety of sizes.

A new bait for this decade that did achieve widespread use was the soft plastic jerkbait. The original, the Slug-Go, was introduced in the early nineties. It quickly developed a reputation as an effective bait. Used spring through fall, the soft plastic jerkbait is usually rigged weightless. A worm hook is threaded through the head and then the point is passed back through the body to lay in a small groove. The hook point is somewhat weedless, but still exposed enough for good hook sets.

Worked around spawning areas, standing timber or above shad schools, baits like the Slug-Go were excellent fish attractors. The undulating, dying minnow appearance of these baits was so effective, many imitators came to the market. Shadows, flukes, Bass Assassins, Senkos and others became common in most anglers' arsenals.

Crankbaits continued their popularity on Table Rock. These hard baits were being offered with bright, reflective, realistic paint jobs. Many crankbaits had life-like, reflective eyes. The colors available seemed to increase every year. In 1997, the Wiggle Wart alone was offered in 98 different color combinations and finishes. Stronger, sharper hooks were being offered on many models.

One of the most successful crankbaits on Table Rock in the 90's was the Storm Wiggle Wart. This plug with a tight wobble runs at medium depths of 4-6 feet. Magnum models will run down to about 10 feet. The Wiggle Wart developed an excellent reputation as a real fish catcher under a variety of conditions and all year long. Its successful use in the B.A.S.S. Missouri Invitational on Table Rock in 1996 only improved the Wart's reputation.

In the early 90's, square-billed crankbaits with a wide wobble began to see use on the lake. One of the first, the Poe's RC3 designed by Rick Clunn, became a popular model. This bait developed a reputation as an effective winter crankbait.

In this decade, crankbaits were available that ran at a variety of depths. The deep running lures (up to a possible 30 feet) were effective on the deep bluff banks of Table Rock. Shallow crankbaits like Mann's Baby 1-Minus and the Timber Tiger found a good following for fishing for shallow and surfacing fish. Lipless crankbaits remained popular for fishing schooled-up bass.

Jerkbaits were being used year-round on the lake. Some of these baits virtually became works of art. Models with highly reflective, realistic finishes were produced by manufacturers like Yamamoto, Yo-Zuri and Lucky Craft. They had to be effective to warrant costs of $15 and more. Some hand crafted jerkbaits cost much more.

Spinnerbaits remained popular on Table Rock. Innovations included reflective skirt materials and titanium shafts. Topwaters continued to see use primarily in specific situations. The best times for surface lures on the lake were post spawn and late fall. Topwaters also maintained their effectiveness at dawn and dusk. Walkers were probably still the most popular topwater. Buzzbaits and chuggers like the Chug Bug saw plenty of use as well.

Live bait continued to be used for all species. Crickets, mealworms and river worms made a good bait for bluegill fishing. Using these natural baits from a shoreline or dock was often the way children caught their first fish from Table Rock. Occasionally, a nice crappie, bass or channel cat was taken with the same method. Minnows remained a good choice for crappie and walleye. Some bass fishermen could take good catches on nightcrawlers, particularly during tough periods in the summer. Nightcrawlers were also used by guides to help their clients catch fish on structure.

Although usually not reflected in creel surveys or electrofishing, trot lining, jug fishing and limb lines remained popular and effective means for taking fish on Table Rock. Just about any species could be caught with these methods, but channel and flathead catfish were most often sought. Using a variety of baits like bluegill, liver, prepared bait and even persimmons, static line angling could produce good eating-sized channels and flatheads up to 50 pounds.

The expansion of fishing tackle and techniques prompted the growth of terminal tackle. Hooks were made in many sizes and styles, particularly for soft plastics. Offset shanks and wide throats became popular for a variety of worms, grubs and tubes. Stronger, sharper treble hooks were incorporated into many crankbaits. Finesse rigs in particular boosted the creation of many new weight designs. Sliding cone-shaped sinkers, eggs weights, split-shot, Mojo weights and bottom walkers were all being used on Table Rock. Under pressure to reduce the use of lead, manufacturers offered weights in brass and tungsten.

The variety of baits and tackle became so great, the need for new tackle storage systems arose. The soft-sided tackle box became a popular method for storing lots of gear in individual, organized boxes or trays within a larger bag. Anglers could sort their baits by type, size or color.

Table Rock anglers used all these baits and techniques in patterns to keep up with changing conditions on the impoundment. Throughout the nineties, fishing became tougher for a variety of reasons. Heavy fishing pressure often made traditional bank pounding methods ineffective. Less visible cover made it more difficult to target fishy areas. Reductions in the largemouth population and increases for Kentuckies and smallmouth necessitated different approaches to bass fishing. Spots and smallies generally prefer deeper water making them more difficult to find and get to. Water quality problems would have an effect on fish populations and activity.

Bill Anderson with the Missouri Department of Conservation has a theory about Table Rock largemouth. He believes it is possible that years of catching largemouth shallow has selectively bred bass that prefer deeper water. Deeper fish are usually harder to catch. Although there is no scientific evidence for this hypothesis, it is an interesting theory about the lake's obviously changing fishery.

Some anglers propose that fish become lure sensitive. After years of seeing spinnerbaits and Wiggle Warts, do they avoid these lures? Table Rock fish do seem to go through periods where they really like a certain bait and then for a few years they ignore it. Again, there is no real evidence to support this theory. Perhaps it's more in the fishermen, his technique and confidence, then in the fish.

The 90's made several things clear on Table Rock. The lake was sensitive to water quality issues. Although able to maintain an excellent fishery for a variety of species, the lake is a limited resource. The lake and its inhabitants undergo natural changes over time. Anglers must be sensitive to these issues, educate themselves and adapt to the lake to continue to maintain a quality fishery.

In the 90's, fishing boats literally extended their size and complexity. The average size of bass boats lengthened with many 20 foot models coming to the market. These bigger craft carried outboards up to 225 hp. Some manufacturers began offering four-stroke engines. Primarily due to the weight and size restrictions of these motors, the four-strokes were not available in sizes greater than 100 hp. They were therefore not suitable for the "big rigs". Almost all large outboards used fuel injection. In the late 90's, FICHT fuel injection was introduced by OMC. Although there were some initial problems with this technology, this innovation became widely used with its improved fuel efficiency and performance and decreased emissions.

Bass boats were increasingly designed for comfort with well cushioned bucket seats and high quality marine carpet. Casting decks increased in size. Models like Gambler were basically all deck with two cockpits. Hydraulic steering made operation easier and safer. In-dash radios and cassette players were common. Due to the high cost of big fiberglass boats, aluminum rigs remained popular. Completely rigged aluminum boats made by Ranger, Lund and Lowe were often seen on Table Rock. The introduction of molded aluminum craft provided a compromise with fiberglass.

Livewells continued to be refined during this period. Concern about fish mortality prompted advances in aeration and continuous recirculation. Table Rock anglers learned that adding salt and ice to livewells improved fish survival. As a guide, 8 lbs. of ice will cool a 30 gal. livewell 10 degrees F. for about three hours. Adding ⅓ cup of noniodized salt per five gallons of water will maintain the proper salinity. Oxygen injection systems became available late in the 90's, but their high price was prohibitive for most Table Rock anglers. By the end of the 1990's, there were only two companies producing trolling motors- Minn Kota and MotorGuide. This did not seem to limit innovation. More powerful models with up to 100 lbs. of thrust on 36 volt systems were available. Minn Kota developed a remote control trolling motor that could be operated from a small wireless keypad.

As trollers got bigger, the need for deep-cycle voltage increased. Most fishing boats had 24 volt systems with some using 36 volt. Proper battery maintenance and charging were more important than ever. To assist with this task, many boats were equipped with on-board chargers. These devices with multi-stage charging made this task simpler, safer and more efficient.

This decade saw the continued refinement of sonar units. Clear, full color screens became available from a greater number of manufacturers. LCD units had almost completely replaced flasher models during the 90's on Table Rock.

Perhaps one of the biggest innovations to improve fishing technology was the GPS unit. Using the Global Positioning System, these hand held devices could identify and store precise locations on the lake. With the use of map software, they could guide an angler back to a "honey hole" or the take-off point. GPS units combined with sonar came to the market late in the 90's.

An interesting development in fishing technology occurred in the late 1990's- the underwater camera. These devices could enable an angler to locate fish and their size and species under docks and in cover. Although not widely used, primarily due to their expense, cameras were an interesting new development in fishing technology. They also raised some ethical questions about their use.

Bass tournaments increased in number and participation on Table Rock during the 90's. There were 263 tournaments with 8,432 boats in 1990 permitted by the Water Patrol. These events peaked in 1997 with 13,085 boats in 335 outings. In 1999, tournaments declined to 283, but still had 12,072 boats participating.

In addition to many smaller club events and larger benefit tourneys, there were some big organized circuits fishing Table Rock. Groups like the Central Pro-Am, Mid-West Outdoorsmen, Red Man and Guys and Gals usually scheduled at least one annual event on this lake. Many of these larger circuits provided formats for professionals and amateurs. Spring was a particularly desirable time to fish "the Rock".

B.A.S.S. held their Missouri Invitational out of Kimberling City in April of 1996 and 1997 and March of 1999. The first three day event was won by Gary Klein with 41 lbs.1 oz. Lee Bailey won in '97 with 47 lbs. 15 oz. It took 58 lbs. 13 oz. for Wayne Crumpton to take top honors in 1999.

One concern that developed from tournaments on Table Rock was that the majority were being held out of the Kimberling City/Hwy. 13 area. This area was popular because of its central location, large marina facilities and availability of services. Many other Table Rock locations were deemed too small to handle several hundred anglers. The concern with this trend was that large numbers of fish wcre being removed throughout the lake and then concentrated around Hwy. 13 upon release. There is evidence that bass do not generally travel very far from their point of release. However, creel and electrofishing studies on Table Rock have not indicated any major shifts in populations which could be attributed to tournaments.

Nevertheless, major tourney organizers have begun releasing fish throughout the lake. Bass are collected from weigh-ins in a large tank on a pontoon boat. The fish are then released from the boat throughout the lake.

Bass tournaments also responded to criticism of fish mortality. In addition to improved handling methods and better livewells, many competitions included quality weigh-in bags, large aerated, treated holding tanks and careful release methods.

When fish are caught deep, over about 30 feet, they will often bloat up from an inflated swim bladder. If these fish are released without deflating the bladder, they will most likely die. As more Kentuckies were caught and deeper techniques were used on Table Rock, bloating became more of a problem. The technique to deflate a fish's swim bladder, called fizzing, requires specific knowledge of fish anatomy. This procedure has become more important as fishermen strive to protect the bass fishery.

Dave Barker has fished Table Rock since the mid-60's. He has adapted well to changes on the lake and has been a very successful tournament angler. Dave started fishing the Central Pro-Am circuit in the early nineties and has qualified for the championship every year since. He has had five first place tournament finishes and won one championship. He was also honored as Central Pro-Am's Angler of the Year three times.

Over the last few years, Barker has refined his skills using deeper and lighter techniques. He likes to fish for bass in flooded cedar groves and around docks with ¼-⁵⁄₁₆ oz. jigs. He also employs grubs on drop-shot rigs with 6 lb. test spinning gear, especially in the clearer water around the dam and in Long Creek. Dave prefers to fish shallow, but will fish up to 65' with gitzits when necessary. His versatility extends to using stickbaits in early spring, worms in the summer and jig-and-eel in the winter. His biggest Table Rock bass, a 10 lb. 2oz. fish, came in April 1990.

Dave Barker continues to be active in the Missouri Bass Club Association, the Guys and Gals circuit with his wife Trudy and the Branson Bass Club.

The 1990's were a period of tremendous growth on Table Rock. Despite the pressure, fishing remained generally good. By the end of the decade, century and millennium, the lake and its fisheries would receive some serious blows.

A nice stringer of warmouth

A Table Rock walleye

An upper White River wiper

Chapter 10
The New Millennium

At the end of the 1990's, water quality and fishing concerns reached a high level on Table Rock Lake. Reduced water clarity, primarily caused by increased levels of algae, disturbed many of those who lived on or visited the lake. In 1999, a largemouth bass kill was documented in different sections of Table Rock. Soon afterward, the presence of Largemouth Bass Virus (LMBV) was detected. In 2001, a state-wide health advisory was issued for possible unacceptable levels of mercury for largemouth bass. In 2002, Table Rock was placed on the List of Impaired Waters by the Missouri Department of Natural Resources. The reason for the listing was nutrient pollution.

Despite these dire occurrences, the lake remained a relatively clear, clean reservoir. Lake use and activity remained high for swimming, skiing, boating and fishing. Although water quality concerns had been voiced for years, the events of the late nineties and early 00's were an indication that this body of water was under assault and sensitive to human encroachment.

The positive facet of these negative occurrences was the attention it brought to protecting and improving the lake. From grassroots groups like the James River Basin Partnership to locally supported organizations like Table Rock Lake Water Quality, Inc. to the federally sponsored Upper White River Water Quality Project, attention, activity and funds were being focused on Table Rock and its watershed.

As the lake moved into its forties, it was having a bit of a midlife crisis. The reduction in largemouth numbers was made worse because mostly bigger bass were lost. However, there were many bright spots in the fishery to help offset this loss. Smallmouth catches seemed to improve and the great population of Kentuckies continued to thrive. The walleye fishing, although limited, was gaining recognition as a quality species. Spoonbills were doing fine and interest in snagging increased. Crappie populations retained their long-time tendency to vary considerably based on annual recruitment. Those who fished for catfish and bluegill continued to find plenty of fish to take their bait.

From 2000 through 2002, Table Rock's lake level averaged below normal pool, mostly due to below normal rainfall. In February 2000, the level reached its lowest point in almost 20 years dipping just below 900'. It rebounded to normal pool by July of the same year. Over the next two years the lake level saw fairly normal fluctuations. The water topped out at over 923' in June, '02.

Discussions continued with the Corps of Engineers over water level issues. Some people advocated higher water levels in the spring maintained until July or August to improve spawning success and recruitment of gamefish. Others promoted periodic draw-downs to increase shoreline vegetation- a process that has been shown to improve fishing.

The Corps has studied a minimum flow project on the White River Reservoirs since 1999. This project would require a permanent increase of about two feet to the normal pool of Table Rock, 1.5 ft. to Beaver and 5 ft. to Bull Shoals. This "extra water" would allow greater average releases through the dams, improving oxygen levels in the tailraces. The most obvious benefit of minimum flows would be improved conditions for trout and other fishes in the areas below the dams, especially on Taneycomo. The tailraces below the big White River dams all have excellent trout fisheries.

The drawback to raising the lakes' normal pools are concerns about increases in high water, shoreline flooding and questions about the ability of the dams to handle potentially higher maximum flood levels.

During the 90's, the Corps evaluated the safety of Table Rock Dam. One outcome of this study was based on new weather data that indicated a probable maximum flood could top the dam by as much as five feet. The original dam design work done in 1948 calculated the maximum potential lake level at 942', five feet below the dam's top. The new rainfall data predicted that catastrophic precipitation could raise the lake to 952' and run over the dam, destroying the earthen embankment portion of the structure. This would cause largescale flooding downstream.

The Corps considered different solutions to this problem including adding ten feet to the top of the dam. This was rejected due to cost and concerns over higher potential lake levels.

The solution they adopted was adding an additional spillway structure on the north side of the dam. This project, the Table Rock Auxiliary Gated Spillway Project, was begun in 2000 and will be completed in 2004 at a cost of $60 million . The new spillway will contain eight gates. If the lake ever rose above 937' (the highest level ever reached is 932.5'), all 18 gates could theoretically be opened with a total maximum release rate of 1,000,000 cubic feet per second. A release of this magnitude could empty Table Rock's total volume of water in less than two days. Let's hope it never rains this much.

The Lakes of Missouri Volunteer Program (LMVP) sampled Table Rock at eighteen sites in 2001 and 2002. The results as indicated in their 2002 Data Report[43] show how difficult it can be to draw trend conclusions from a limited number of years. In 2001, five sites changed from mesotrophic to oligotrophic based on chlorophyll values. In 2002, 11 of the sites tested increased their productivity level. The reasons for these dramatic shifts over a fairly short period are not fully understood. Natural cycles of algae productivity and weather conditions are probably primary determinants. Heavy spring rains in 2002 created large amounts of runoff from the watershed raising the lake to 923 feet. There was considerable algae present in Table Rock following these rains and throughout the rest of the year.

In the first years of the new millennium, several projects began to address water quality concerns in the White River basin. The placing of Table Rock on the List of Impaired Waters required the Department of Natural Resources to determine the cause for excessive nutrients in the lake and develop a plan to correct the condition.

In December, 2002, the Missouri Attorney General announced a "zero tolerance initiative" for pollution issues affecting the White River watershed. Jay Nixon vowed to vigorously prosecute water pollution violators saying, "zero tolerance is the step we need to take to protect the lakes and streams in this area for now and for future generations".

Missouri Congressman Blunt and Senators Bond and Talent helped secure funding for the Upper White River Water Quality Project in early 2003. This project would provide support to local activities improving the area's water quality. The funding also provided $1 million for facility improvements on Table Rock Lake including campground and boat ramp upgrades. Municipalities in the Table Rock watershed continued to upgrade their sewage treatment plants to meet state and federal mandates.

The die-off of black bass in 1999 had a significant impact on the perceptions of anglers. It is not unusual for some fish to die from stress and disease, particularly in the heat of late summer. Surface temperatures can sometimes reach 90 degrees F. on Table Rock and oxygen levels are lower in warmer water. Cold-blooded fish require more oxygen when the water is warmer. These conditions can put fish in a stressful situation and lead to mortality. Bass are particularly prone to oxygen deficiency.

The fish kill on Table Rock in 1999 seemed to affect the bigger largemouth the most, but spots and smallmouth were also involved. Fish collected by the Department of Conservation were examined and found to have lesions caused by the parasite *Epistylis*. The lesions created an infection route for bacteria that eventually caused the fishes' death from septicemia. At least a year prior to the documented fish kill, anglers had been noticing red sores on black bass.

In 1999, tissue samples from Table Rock largemouth bass tested positive for Largemouth Bass Virus (LMBV). This viral infection has been detected in many large reservoirs throughout the south and mid-west. LMBV can infect all black bass, but seems to be most fatal to big largemouth. This disease is not completely understood yet. It appears to affect the swim bladder of bass and have the greatest impact on older fish that may already be stressed.

LMBV does not always kill fish. It is not harmful to humans.

So far, bass populations that have experienced LMBV have rebounded within two or three years. It appears that the disease has a short-lived impact on a fishery. Several state organizations and the U.S. Fish and Wildlife Service are studying this disease. There is no known cure or treatment and presently there are no plans to change regulations to counter LMBV on Table Rock.

In 2001 a state-wide mercury health advisory was issued for largemouth bass. Under the advisory, children under 12 years old and women who are or may become pregnant or are nursing were advised to not eat largemouth bass over 12 inches in length. This advisory was issued in part due to the EPA reducing the acceptable level of mercury in fish from 1000 ppb to 300 ppb. Despite the fact that bass samples from Table Rock did not exceed the new limit (tests in 2001 showed an average level of 238 ppb), this advisory furthered the perception that Table Rock's fishery was in trouble.

Fishing did seem to suffer as the lake greeted a new millennium. Angling in general was tough and fewer big bass were caught. Interest in fishing did seem to decrease and some anglers became frustrated with reduced catches.

The bass diseases were definitely a contributor to this malaise. However, there were probably many other factors involved. Spawning success, recruitment, water clarity and hot, dry temperatures certainly affected fishing. Anglers had to adapt to fishing more for Kentuckies and smallmouth and less for largemouth bass. This trend had been developing for years on Table Rock. Some anglers adapted well; some did not.

As always, fisheries go through natural cycles and the angler must adjust to them. Failure to do so will cause poorer fishing results. These events were a reminder that we need to be very vigilant about protecting the remarkable natural resources of Table Rock Lake.

As Table Rock started a new century, the Missouri Department of Conservation continued electrofishing on four areas of the lake.[44] These studies performed during the black bass spawn were done in the James, Kings, Long Creek and on the White between Campbell

Point and Kimberling City.

In 2000, all four testing locations showed good numbers of largemouth and spotted bass. The Kings and James had the largest capture rates of largemouth over 8" long recorded in several years. In the White and Long Creek, largemouth numbers were down some and Kentuckies had increased. Crappie numbers measured in the Kings and James were low, but comparable to the previous several years.

In 2001, black bass numbers were down at all locations electrofished. Some of this reduction can be attributed to clear water conditions. The clear water apparently caused fish to spawn deeper making them less vulnerable to shocking. 2002 electrofishing showed largemouth numbers down at all four locations sampled. Spotted bass were up at all sites except the James. In the mid-White, capture rates were higher for spots than largemouth. The average size of black bass electrofished showed some improvement. High water conditions during the late spring and early summer of 2002 were hoped to encourage good spawning success.

Crappie were only sampled in the James in 2002. Numbers were improved over the previous several years. Throughout 2002, anecdotal reports from fishermen were positive on the numbers and size of crappie in Table Rock.

Surprisingly, the electrofishing results for black bass from 1999 to 2002 did not reveal decreased numbers of fish over 15 inches. This was completely contrary to anecdotal reports, angler interviews and tournament results. Perhaps the electrofishing data tended to favor largemouth due to their penchant for shallower spawning.

Sampling for walleye in the upper Kings in 2000 was hampered by low water levels. 2001 testing was more successful. Both years' data show a healthy population of walleyes running up the Kings each spring. The ratio of fish over the 18" minimum length limit was very good. Efforts to electrofish walleye in the James continued to be unsuccessful.

In 2002, one night of electrofishing for walleye in the upper Kings produced good numbers of quality fish. This was the first year that efforts were made to electrofish walleye in the dam area. A few were captured verifying that walleye were indeed in this part of the lake. Although generally smaller, these walleye showed very good growth rates. An effort to shock walleye in the James yielded no fish.

The Missouri Department of Conservation planned to start stocking walleye in the James in 2002. Due to a production failure at the hatchery, this project was delayed. Starting in 2003, 90,000 2-inch walleye fingerlings will be released into the James each year for three years. With its similarities to the Kings, it was hoped that this project would establish a sustainable population in this area.

For several years, the Department of Conservation has captured brood stock walleye from the Kings during electrofishing. These male and female fish are transferred to the Chesapeake State Fish Hatchery in Chesapeake, Missouri. Milt and eggs are collected at the hatchery to produce several thousand walleye fry each year. The walleye fry are raised to fingerling size and then used for stocking programs throughout Missouri including Bull Shoals, Stockton and Table Rock. The walleye stocked into Table Rock are from the Table Rock broodstock.

Broodstock fish are returned to Table Rock in a specially designed fish hauling truck. This vehicle has several holding tanks designed to minimize jostling of the fish. The tanks are filled with spring water from the hatchery. Salt is added at 0.5% to help sedate and protect the fish. The tanks have aeration, temperature control and oxygen injection. Every effort is made to protect this valuable, productive resource.

The Chesapeake State Fish Hatchery was built by the CCC during the 1930's and completely remodeled in the 80's. In addition to walleye, the facility raises largemouth bass, channel and flathead catfish, bluegill, sunfish and minnows for stocking programs throughout Missouri.

In 2002, the Arkansas Game & Fish Commission stocked 8,400 walleye fingerlings into Cricket Creek, a tributary of Long Creek. They also documented a significant walleye spawning run up the White River below Beaver.

After Beaver dam was built, the Arkansas Game & Fish Commission worked to establish a trout population in the tailwaters. Trout have done well in the areas below all the White River dams. Starting in 1966, they stocked rainbow trout below Beaver. In the mid-80's, brown trout were stocked in this area and in the early 90's, brook and cutthroat trout were released. On-going stockings have created an excellent put-and-take fishery in this area of the White River. In 2003, the Commission planned to release 122,000 rainbows, 10,000 browns, 20,000 cutthroat and 6,000 brook trout. These trout were all of the 11 inch size.

The trout making up this fishery tend to stay in the cold, fast-moving water of the very upper end of Table Rock. Some of them probably migrate to other areas of the lake, but the best trout fishing on Table Rock would be in the Arkansas portion of the lake above Beaver Town.

The Department of Conservation performed gill netting for paddlefish in March of 2000 and 2001. Good numbers of large paddlefish were collected. Effective March 1, 2000, the minimum legal length for paddlefish was changed from 24" to 34", measured from eye to tail fork. In 2001, almost 15,000 paddlefish fingerlings were stocked in Table Rock.

Angler surveys were conducted during the spring snagging season on the James in 2001 and 2002. An estimated 1,257 spoonbill averaging 39.5 inches were harvested in 2001. 2002 was even better with the highest estimated harvest ever recorded of 1,368 averaging 40.8 inches. Angling effort was very high both years with 4,197 snaggers exerting 20,613 hours of fishing in 2001 and 3,996 fishing 21,972 hours in 2002. Definite skill is required for this sport as 25% of the anglers account for the full harvest.

On 3/15/02, George Russell snagged a Missouri state record paddlefish of 139 lbs. 4oz. in the James near Cape Fair. This widely publicized feat spurred the interest in spoonbill snagging.

Changes in Table Rock's bass fishery affected the way many anglers approached the sport. It was becoming increasingly necessary to use deeper and more finesse tactics to be successful. With fewer largemouth and more spots and smallmouth being caught, different baits, techniques and patterns were called for.

Carolina-, drop-shot, split-shot and do-nothing rigs grew in popularity. Soft plastic baits were generally downsized with French fries, Zoom worms, razor worms and small grubs and tube baits used frequently. One exception to this trend was the introduction of creature baits. Soft plastics with numerous appendages presented a tempting profile when bass could be found shallow. Snap-back plastics were introduced with tougher, tear resistant, floating features.

Structure fishing became more important as fishermen found they needed to fish somewhat deeper throughout most of the year. Anglers who could locate brush piles, humps, channel bends or the ends of long points had a better chance of catching fish, particularly Kentuckies.

Many lures, both hard and soft, continued the trend toward realistic finishes. Reflective finishes and eyes were common on many baits. Hard baits were still used on Table Rock, but were most successful in specific patterns. The spawning period and the fall were the best times to employ crankbaits and spinnerbaits. Occasionally, a warm spell in the winter would provide a good opportunity for wide-wobbling crankbaits like the RC-3 or Fat Free Shad on rocky shorelines. Topwater lures were not productive during the first couple years of the 21st century on Table Rock.

The jerkbait did retain its popularity and effectiveness. Once considered a bait primarily for the late-winter and pre-spawn periods, these plugs were producing year-round. Using variations of the jerk-pause method and employing floating, suspending and sinking models, jerkbaits performed well throughout the lake on all three sub-species of bass. These baits would also take walleye when trolled across large gravel flats in the Kings and upper White arms. Quality walleye were also caught in the upper Kings during the winter by trolling live minnow rigs.

Deep techniques continued to take bass during the '00s, particularly in summer and winter. Using their graphs, anglers would locate fish off points, along channels and on deep gravel banks. Jerking spoons or tailspinners in depths of 20-100 ft. could produce decent catches. Jerking spoons is generally done on medium to heavy baitcasting equipment. The lure is dropped down over graphed fish, usually to the bottom. The bait is reeled up slightly, snapped up with the rod and then allowed to flutter back down. Fish will usually take the bait on the fall, so keeping in touch with the line is important.

Fishing the same types of deep locations with light gear was also successful. Using light line, often on spinning tackle, small lead-head jigs dressed with a small plastic grub or tube bait were let down to fish on likely deep structure or cover. Light jigging usually required a sensitive approach with little or no movement of the bait. This technique was particularly effective on Kentuckies.

Ralph Lambert is especially adept at light jigging. After fishing the lake for more than 40 years, he knows many isolated locations with good structure and/or cover. He often finds these spots in the Kings and White by triangulating to shoreline landmarks. Ralph favors long point ends, channel edges, humps and tree lines. He fishes fairly deep 20-45' using 6lb. test line on spinning outfits. Using hand-poured jig heads with the barb removed and a 4-6" worm or French fry, Ralph can often limit out on Kentuckies just about any time of year.

One drawback to these deep techniques was they tended to cause fish to bloat. A fish caught at a depth of 30 feet or greater will almost always bloat up. Bringing a fish up slowly sometimes helped reduce this problem. The technique of "fizzing" would possibly save a fish if performed properly. A bass of less than 15 inches, if released bloated, would almost certainly die. Legal bloated fish should be harvested if not "deflated".

Crappie fishing remained sporadic on Table Rock during this period. They were hard to locate in any numbers, but the quality of the fish was good. Fishing during the spawn or near docks or brush piles produced the best crappie fishing. The continued decline in visible cover made crappie fishing more challenging. Minnows and small crappie jigs remained the best baits for this species.

White bass continued to be a popular sport fish on Table Rock. The spring runs up the Kings, James, White and Long Creek produced good catches of whites in 2000 and 2001. Starting around March 1st, anglers caught these migrating fish by trolling crankbaits or small spinners along the channels and on deeper flats. The 2002 run was sporadic, possibly due to inconsistent spring weather conditions. A new state record white of 5 lb. 6oz. was caught on Table Rock by Scott Flood on March 19, 2002.

Throughout the summer and into the fall, schools of whites were targeted in deeper water or in coves when chasing large schools of threadfin shad in Table Rock. Finding a feeding frenzy of whites could produce some fast and furious action on this scrappy fish.

Some stripers and wipers (a cross between a striper and white bass) exist in the upper end of the White River on Table Rock. These fish have come into the lake from Beaver and do not appear to have spread throughout the lake. They provide another unique fishery for the reservoir. In 2000, Jeff Fletcher caught an Arkansas state record striper of 64 lbs. 8oz. on the upper White.

Live bait did see some increase in use during the early 2000's. Live minnows, worms and crawfish had always been effective baits, but the generally tough fishing conditions during this period made them more popular. Fishing guides in particular, who needed to find catchable fish fast for their clients, sometimes resorted to live bait for its effectiveness.

Changing conditions on Table Rock Reservoir required anglers to become even more reliant on technology. Graphs especially were a necessity for locating deep structure, shad schools and concentrations of fish. The continuing improvement in sonar technology display made deeper fishing easier. Sonar units included numerous additional features including GPS, water temperature, boat speed and barometric pressure. Smart Cast introduced a wireless transducer that could be placed or cast in one location and read from another.

Trolling motors were still an integral tool of Table Rock anglers. The use of Carolina- and drop-shot rigs often required sustained slow trolling. Deep techniques necessitated pin-point control to stay along or over structure. Although expensive, some fishermen could choose wireless controls and motorized deploy and stow features on their trolling motors.

GPS units improved their usefulness. Hand-held models or ones combined with a sonar unit could display lake maps and provide location and directions. In March of 2002, Bass Pro Shop held a tournament out of Hwy. 13. On the second day, a snowstorm caught

133

the contestants on the lake in blizzard conditions. Some had to use their GPS units to find their way back to the launch site. This tournament did produce good results with some nice bags of quality bass. The leading weight on the first day was 25.85 lbs. It took 17.95 lbs. on the second day to win, despite the snow.

As with many new technologies, over time, acceptance of underwater cameras as a fishing aid increased somewhat. Although not widely used, cameras were becoming another effective tool for locating fish, particularly for tournament anglers and guides. Livewell technology was improved with the introduction of small solid state oxygenators. Continued refinements in livewells and fish handling methods were important conservation improvements.

The bass boat seemed to be peaking out in size at about 22' and 300 hp. They did get wider with beams up to 92" providing more stability, storage and deck space. Concerns over fuel efficiency and emissions continued to propel 4-stroke development, but their use on bigger craft was very limited. The EPA's mandate to lower hydrocarbon emissions 75% by 2006 spurred continued refinement of direct fuel injection systems.

The number of fishing tournaments on Table Rock fell in 2000 to 219 events, the lowest since 1983. There were still 10,555 boats involved. There were 263 and 257 permitted competitions in 2001 and 2002 respectively. The reason for the decrease in tournaments is unknown, but it is most likely due to negative reports on water quality and specifically the largemouth die-off in 1999.

B.A.S.S. held invitational events on Table Rock in April of 2000 and 2001. Jim Dopp won the 2000, 3 day tournament with 39 lbs. 5oz. Jay Yelas brought in 43 lbs. 13oz. to win the 2001 event.

Bass tournaments continued to see good numbers of fish weighed in, however total weights and big bass weights were down. Many tournaments were won with a limit of Kentuckies with an occasional quality smallmouth or largemouth brought in. Big bass weights were a definitive indicator of the loss of the bigger largemouth. Many competitions were won with big bass weighing less than five pounds.

The bright side was that many quality spotted bass of 2-4 lbs. and an increasing number of nice smallies were being brought in. Whether this was due to the available fishes or the techniques used is unclear. Probable a little of both.

Weigh-in results from two major circuits reflect the change in the size of bass brought in. Heartland and Central Pro-Am held major events on Table Rock in 1999 through 2002. These organizations attract over 100 boats and some of the best anglers around. The following results for tournaments held between February and June show how total weights and big bass weights declined after 1999. Results for early 2003 showed some improvement with the average size of Kentuckies increasing and more bigger largemouth showing up.

Circuit	Date	Heavy Stringer lbs. 5 fish	Big Bass	Big Bass Over 5 lbs.
Heartland	2/28/99	28.16	7.78	9
Heartland	4/16/00	15.40	7.2	3
Heartland	4/8/01	15.95	5.54	4
Heartland	4/14/02	16.32	5.28	2
C P-A	6/6/99	20.4	6.35	42
C P-A	6/19/99	25.7	7.75	38
C P-A	3/25/00	17.65	7.05	21
C P-A	6/4/00	16.00	6.60	21
C P-A	4/28/01	18.65	4.70	0
C P-A	4/27/02	18.00	5.75	-
C P-A	6/8/02	22.75	5.80	-

In 2001, Missouri and Arkansas introduced the White River Border Lakes Permit. This permit allowed anglers with a Missouri or Arkansas resident fishing license to fish Bull Shoals, Norfolk and Table Rock Lakes on either side of the state line. The $10 annual permit made it possible for fishermen from these two states to fish all the impounded portions of these lakes without buying an out-of-state license. Arkansas' length limit on spotted bass is 12 inches. These bass can be possessed on Arkansas waters, but not in Missouri.

The White River is a tremendous fishery. Native Americans speared fish in it. Early settlers trapped fish. Early 20th century fishermen developed the float trip and employed various angling methods to entice fish.

When the dream of Table Rock Reservoir was realized in 1959, its development as a fishery was not of primary importance. But the lake blossomed and became one of the most attractive fishing locations in America.

Table Rock angling has brought enjoyment to millions. From a child's first bluegill to a tournament angler's first place bag to an elderly fisherman's 50 pound flathead on a trot line, this lake continues to produce, challenge and inspire.

Author's son with a 2001 bass caught on a jerkbait

Jeff Fletcher's Arkansas record striper

The author with a walleye

Chapter 11
The Future

The views expressed in this chapter are the personal opinions of the author. The fishermen interviewed for this book all expressed cautious optimism about the future of fishing on Table Rock. There is a great amount of interest in protecting this resource. Continued work by the Missouri Department of Conservation and Department of Natural Resources should help assure good water quality and habitat for the fishery. Local residents and public officials recognize the importance of Table Rock as a beautiful natural resource and economic generator. As a vacation and retirement destination, the Table Rock area will undoubtably continue to grow. Increased human development will be an ongoing challenge for Table Rock Lake.

Work being done by the Corps of Engineers will likely result in slightly higher water levels. With the completion of the spillway project and minimum flow studies, it is probable that the normal pool for Table Rock will be raised one or two feet. There are indications that the Corps may give more consideration to sustaining water levels during fish spawning periods. However, there are so many factors affecting lake levels, this may be difficult to achieve on any regular basis.

The Department of Conservation has invested considerable work and study in Table Rock since its impoundment. This work will surely continue with emphasis on sustaining existing populations. Indications are that the largemouth population will rebound and that bigger fish will become more prevalent. There are some indications of this from anecdotal reports and tournament results in early 2003. The Kentucky population is in excellent shape and this species should continue to do well. Smallmouth will probably remain a small, but quality resource. It would be interesting to see if smallmouth fishing could be evaluated and improved on the upper ends of the major tributaries.

Electrofishing will probably remain the major source of fish population estimates. It might be helpful to incorporate an occasional creel survey to offset some of the inherent drawbacks to electrofishing data. Surveys also would provide information on a wider variety of fishes.

Crappie fishing will continue to vary based on annual recruitment. A study to determine the causes of this variation would be helpful in determining if a more stable crappie population could be supported. Perhaps largescale habitat development as instituted on lakes like Stockton would at least provide anglers with better opportunities.

The walleye fishery should continue to do well and attract more interest from anglers. Efforts to establish a self-sustaining population of walleye in the James should be successful. The James is so similar to the Kings, walleye will hopefully find this area as hospitable.

The paddlefish will do well in the James as long as the hatchery program is successful and poaching can be controlled or eradicated. Since spoonbill have been documented in all areas of the lake, it will be interesting to see if they might begin to reproduce in other areas of the lake.

The put-and-take trout fishery established in Beaver's tailwaters by the Arkansas Game & Fish Commission has been very successful and will probably attract more attention. The presence of rainbow, brown, cutthroat and brook trout should be irresistible to serious trout fishermen.

White bass will do well in Table Rock as long as the shad populations remain healthy. It is possible that more reports of striped bass will occur in the future. These fish are already in Table Rock and their preferred habitat is certainly available.

Based on present situations, there are no known planned fishing regulation changes. If largemouth don't rebound as expected, public demand for specific protection for this sub-species might occur. Special length limits or protection for largemouth during the spawn might be considered if anglers become frustrated due to fewer large bass. Proposals to reduce spotted bass length limits have faded. It is doubtful this will occur unless it is determined that the Kentuckies have limited largemouth numbers through competition.

Water quality will remain a major issue on Table Rock. Conditions should improve as phosphorus removal is brought on-line at more treatment plants. Improvements in septic system design will hopefully at least stabilize this non-point source of pollution. It is imperative that cooperative efforts between Missouri and Arkansas continue to improve watershed issues affecting both states. Specifically, the Kings River arm requires attention now. Failure to control nutrient input on the Kings could result in hyper-eutrophic conditions developing.

The great amount of attention and effort focused on Table Rock water quality issues will no doubt continue and result in some improvements. It would be particularly promising to see some water issues resolved in the upper James. Excessive bacteria has caused some unfortunate advisories against swimming in this stream. This situation has created both economic and esthetic difficulties for this area.

Within the next few years, it is possible that some concerns will be expressed about the lack of nutrients in some areas of the reservoir. Healthy nutrient loads are necessary for a viable fishery. If efforts to remove these nutrients are too successful, ultimately Table Rock's fish populations could suffer.

Concerns over health advisories for mercury and lead will be difficult to resolve. One source of such contaminants is air pollution- a complicated source to control. Scientific studies may continue to force lower limits on some contaminants. Some heavy metals take long periods to move up the food chain. It is likely that health advisories for certain fish, especially bass, catfish and spoonbill will continue to occur.

Fishing equipment will improve in design and sophistication. New baits will become popular and old ones will fall out of favor. Periodically, some older baits will come back into fashion. Wooden plugs, prop baits and surface commotion lures like the Hula Popper or Jitterbug are possible candidates. Plastic offerings, particularly for finesse approaches, will remain very popular. Although the general trend is toward smaller baits, larger soft plastic lures will find specific uses.

Rods and reels will exploit technology to become more useful. Reels with improved backlash control, line measurement and speed indication are likely. Improved materials will make rods stronger, lighter and faster. Electronics will continue the trend of clearer displays and combination uses with GPS and perhaps wireless communication. It would be exciting to see a graph that could identify fish species. Underwater cameras will become more widely accepted.

Angling techniques on Table Rock will most likely continue their move to finesse and deeper tactics. There is no doubt many successful Table Rock anglers are using these approaches to catch more fish and win tournaments. If the largemouth population rebounds well, it might improve success rates for more shallow fishing. Lake clarity will also affect presentations. If Table Rock becomes darker, there may be a trend by both fish and fishermen to move shallower. If the lake becomes clearer through water quality controls, the deeper techniques will become even more important.

It is doubtful that the standard bass boat will get much bigger. There does not seem to be any reason to increase the size any more. With emission controls, the four-stroke engine will become common. The greater size and weight of 4-strokes may limit their practical use as outboards on the larger rigs.

Trolling motors will become smarter and easier to use. Self-deployment and retraction, remote wireless control and maybe even voice-activated control will become more common. Boat interiors will be made more comfortable, safe and protective. Custom designs for a particular angler's style may be available. Livewell technology will improve with built-in temperature control, oxygen and additive injection and fish capture devices.

Tournaments will continue on Table Rock. There will be many and they will be large. If the fish are here, they will come. There might be more smaller tournaments available as some anglers tire of the size, competitiveness and expense of the big tourneys. As the boomers age, this may be a factor in the desire for simpler, smaller events. It would be nice to see tournaments spread throughout the lake area more. Although Hwy. 13 obviously has the location and amenities for large tournaments, other areas of Table Rock could also support and benefit from some of these events. This would also help dispel perceptions about concentrating fish in the mid-lake area. Non-professional tournaments might want to experiment with using fish length measurement and eliminate weigh-ins.

This writer feels that there may be a trend developing away from technology and a return to simpler methods. The use of smaller boats, antique tackle and no electronics might be desirable to some fishermen. Partly due to expense and partly to a desire for simpler, more sporting methods, there seems to be an underlying need for basic fishing. It is possible that some angling has become so expensive and technical that children and young people can't afford it or can't master it. If we fail to pass this sport on to our children in a way they can enjoy, they won't embrace it. The quality of Table Rock Lake as a resource and a fishery will depend to a large extent on how we treat it now and how we teach our children and grandchildren to treat it.

God created the beautiful White River. Man has altered it dramatically. There have been successes and there have been mistakes. Ultimately, we have the responsibility for stewardship of Table Rock. It will become what we make of it.

Future Table Rock angler

End Notes

1. Goodspeed, <u>Goodspeed's 1888 History of Barry County,</u> The Goodspeed Publishing Co., 1888
2. Ibid
3. <u>The Taney Co. Republican,</u> July 16, 1896
4. Ingenthron, Elmo, <u>The Land of Taney,</u> 1974
5. Sullivan, K.C., <u>Biological Notes on James River and Shoal Creek, Missouri,</u> Missouri State Game and Fish Department, 1933
6. Goodspeed, <u>Goodspeed's 1888 History of Barry County,</u> The Goodspeed Publishing Co., 1888
7. <u>The Taney Co. Republican,</u> September 18, 1963
8. <u>The Springfield Mirror,</u> February, 1929
9. Dam construction details provided by Carl Garner, Assistant Chief of Engineering during Table Rock Dam construction
10. Sullivan, K.C., <u>Biological Notes on James River and Shoal Creek, Missouri,</u> Missouri State Game and Fish Department, 1933
11. Colvin, Michael A., <u>Evaluation of Minimum Size Limits and Reduced Daily Limits of the Crappie Population and Fisheries in Five Large Missouri Impoundments,</u> Missouri Department of Conservation, 1991
12. Hanson, William D., <u>Harvest of Fish in Table Rock Reservoir,</u> Missouri Department of Conservation, 1974
13. Hanson, William D., <u>Harvest of Fish in Selected Areas of Table Rock Reservoir,</u> Missouri Department of Conservation, 1971
14. Ibid
15. Ibid
16. Ibid
17. Hanson, William D., <u>Harvest of Fish in Table Rock Reservoir,</u> Missouri Department of Conservation, 1974
18. Dieffenbach, William and Ryck, Frank Jr., <u>Water Quality Survey of the Elk, James and Spring River Basins of Missouri,</u> 1964-1965, Missouri Department of Conservation, 1976

19. Reprinted from the book, "Ridge Runner, From the Big Piney to the Battle of the Bulge", author Larry Dablemont, Lightnin' Ridge Books, Box 22, Bolivar, Missouri, 65613

20. Colvin, Michael A., <u>Evaluation of Minimum Size Limits and Reduced Daily Limits of the Crappie Population and Fisheries in Five Large Missouri Impoundments</u>, Missouri Department of Conservation,1991

21. Graham, L. Kim, <u>Establishing and Maintaining Paddlefish Populations by Stocking,</u> Missouri Department of Conservation, 1986

22. Hanson, William D., <u>Harvest of Fish in Selected Areas of Table Rock Reservoir,</u> Missouri Department of Conservation, 1971

23. Hanson, William D., <u>Harvest of Fish in Table Rock Reservoir,</u> Missouri Department of Conservation, 1974

24. Novinger, Gary D., <u>Evaluation of a 15.0-Inch Minimum Length Limit on Largemouth Bass and Spotted Bass Catches at Table Rock Lake, Missouri,</u> Missouri Department of Conservation, 1987

25. Ibid

26. Ibid

27. Ibid

28. Ming, Arvil, <u>A Study of Black Bass Fishing Tournaments in Missouri,</u> Missouri Department of Conservation, 1977

29. Colvin, Michael A., <u>Evaluation of Minimum Size Limits and Reduced Daily Limits of the Crappie Population and Fisheries in Five Large Missouri Impoundments,</u> Missouri Department of Conservation, 1991

30. Anderson, William M., <u>Table Rock Lake Annual Reports,</u> Missouri Department of Conservation, 1987-1989

31. Novinger, Gary D., <u>Evaluation of a 15.0-Inch Minimum Length Limit on Largemouth Bass and Spotted Bass Catches at Table Rock Lake, Missouri,</u> Missouri Department of Conservation, 1987

32. Anderson, William M., <u>Table Rock Lake Annual Reports,</u> Missouri Department of Conservation,1984-89

33. Graham, L. Kim, <u>Establishing and Maintaining Paddlefish</u>

Populations by Stocking, Misoouri Department of
Conservation, 1986
34. Anderson, William M., Table Rock Lake Annual Reports,
Missouri Department of Conservation, 1986-90 and
Novinger, Gary D., Evaluation of a 15.0-Inch Minimum
Length Limit on Largemouth Bass and Spotted Bass Catches
at Table Rock Lake, Missouri, Missouri Deparment of
Conservation, 1987
35. Anderson, William M., Table Rock Lake Annual Report,
Missouri Department of Conservation, 1990
36. Missouri Department of Conservation website
37. Anderson, William M., Table Rock Lake Annual Reports,
Missouri Department of Conservation, 1990-99
38. Ibid
39. Anderson, William M., Table Rock Lake Annual Report,
Missouri Department of Conservation, 1992
40. Obrecht, D.V., Pope, F.E., Thorpe, A.P. and Jones, J.R.,
Lakes of Missouri Volunteer Program Data Reports,
1992-2000
41. Hanson, William D., Harvest of Fish in Selected Areas of
Table Rock Reservoir, Missouri Department of
Conservation, 1971 and Harvest of Fish in Table Rock
Reservoir, Missouri Department of Conservation, 1974 and
Novinger, Gary D., Recruitment of Largemouth and Spotted
Bass at Table Rock Lake, Missouri Department of
Conservation, 1988
42. Obrecht, D.V., Thorpe, A.P. and Jones, J.R., Lakes of
Missouri Volunteer Program Data Reports, 2001-2002
43. Ibid.
44. Anderson, William M., Table Rock Lake Annual Report,
Missouri Department of Conservation, 2002

<u>Devil's Pool, A History of Big Cedar Lodge,</u> Charlie Farmer, JLM Publishing Co., Springfield, Missouri, 1995

<u>Indians and Archaeology of Missouri,</u> Carl H. And Eleanor F. Chapman, University of Missouri Press, 1983 edition

<u>Indians of the Ozark Plateau,</u> Elmo Ingenthron, 1970

<u>Ozark Mountain Country</u>, Frank Reuter, ed., White Oak Press, 1972

<u>Some Recollections of an Ozarks Float Trip Guide,</u> Ted Sare, Webster Co. Printing, 1997

<u>The Land of Taney,</u> Elmo Ingenthron, 1974

<u>The Ozarks Land and Life,</u> Milton D. Rafferty, University of Oklahoma Press, 1980

<u>White River,</u> Frank Amato Publications

Index

Agitator lure 71
algae 102,107,109,123,125
Allison Craft 95
Ambassador reel 19,60,70,79,84,98
Anderson, Bill 73,89,90,97,116
Bacon, Basil.. 22,70
Barker, Dave 60,75,120
Barnes, Charlie 15,16,17,19
Bass Pro Shop 14,64,133
bass, black, daily limit 66
bass, black, length limit 53,66,67,69,89,97,104, 139
Baxter.. 32,34,98,108
Beaver Town 21,33,41
Beck, Bill... 98-9
Berryville, Ar. 44,110
Big Creek 6,89
Big Indian Creek.................................... 6,24,32,90,103
Big M... 24,32,51,58
black lights..87
Bomber bait..57,60,73,81,98
boron rods 85
Branson 15,16,26,30,41,63,106,110
Bread Tray Mountain.. 34
buffalo.. 49
Buffalo River 16
Bunch, Larry 19,21
buried treasure 34
buttons... 4
buzzbait 72,115
cameras, underwater 118,134,140
Campbell Point 32,54,81,85,127
Campbell, Charlie.......................14,60,78-80,85,94,100
Cape Fair 10,24,32,35,41,63
Carolina-rig..................................111,112,113,130,133
carp.. 6,8,49,54

Cassville 56,110
catfish, blue 49
catfish, bullhead 49
caves 33-4,47
CCC 13,129
cemetery relocation 32
Central Pro-Am 119,120,135
Chesapeake State Fish Hatchery 129
chlordane 105,107
Clunn, Rick 94,115
Color-C-Lector 94
Colvin, Michael A 51,65,89
Conservation sales tax 97
Cow Creek 23,30,32,33
crappie, daily limit 51,65,84,89
crappie, length limit 51,65,89
crawfish 10,68
Dablemont, Norton 58
Dance, Bill 75
darters 5,49
Devil's Pool 13-4,78,79
Dick, Rube 21,44
Dieffenbach, William 55-6
Dixie Jet Flutter Spoon 74,98,99
Dixon, Denver 58
docks 33,83,89
drop-shotting 98,112,113,130,133
drum 6,49
Eagle Rock 6,16,21,23,24,32,34,35,41,43,51,63,82,102,106
eels 16
Electro Pal 77
electrofishing technique 67-8,138
Elk River 55
eminent domain 30
Ensley, Harold 22,62,94
eutrophication process 102,108
fecal coliform bacteria 56

ferries 23,24,42,44
finesse tactics 98,103,111-2,140
Finley River 9,10,16,56
fish kill 11,123,126,134
fish traps...10
fizzing 120,132
Flat Creek 21-2,16,17
Fletcher, J.D. 6,8,19,20,21-2,54,62,72,121,122
Fletcher, Jeff..22,133,136
flipping technique 70-1,111,113
flowage easements 29,30
fluorescent line..87
Foster, Ralph..16,22
four-stroke engines.................................117,134,140
Galena Boat Company 15,18
gar 49,54
Garland, Bobby 98
gigging 6,8,9
Gitzit 85,98,120
Global Positioning Position(GPS) 118,134,140
Goat Hill 43
goggle-eye...10,16,49
Golden Gate Bridge 41
Goodspeed...3,12
Graham, Kim L. 65,91
graphite rods.................................... 22,70,85,111
Guys & Gals...119,120
hand grabbing 9
hand lines 5
Hanson, William D. 51,52,53,54,66
hatcheries 12,41,53,129
Heartland..135
Hellbender.. 57,73,97
Hibdon, Guido 85
Hill, Dr, Loren 87
Hollister..4,24
Humminbird flasher 77

Hydra Sports 95
Ingenthron, Elmo 10
jack salmon 16
Jakes Branch 24,43
James River Basin Partnership 123
Joe Bald...32,34,80
johnboat..............5,6,11,15,16,17,19,20,21,59,61,87
Johnson reels...21,56
karst topography 46
Kimberling City 23,41,42,63,110,119,128
Kimberling ferry 23,42
King, Stacey..94
Kinsey Craft..78
Klein, Gary...119
lake depth..35,124
lake level, highest 50
lake level, lowest 50
Lakes of Missouri Volunteer
Program(LMVP)..107-9,125
Lambert, Ralph 50,57,112,132
Langley, Dan...71
Largemouth Bass Virus(LMBV) 123,126-7
Lea, Wallace 10,80-1
lead...107,116,139
Liquid Crystal Graph(LCG)........................93,118
List of Impaired Waters 123,125
Little Green Box flasher 71,77,98
lost mines 34
Lowrance, Carl 77
lure sensitivity.......................................81,116-7
Mano 44
Mark Twain National Forest.............................30
Martin, Gene 89
meanmouth..103
mercury 107,123,127,139
Mid-America Bass Fishermen's Association............76
Mid-West Outdoorsmen.................................119

Ming, Arvil...76
minimum flow project 124,137
MinnKota 118
Moon Glow 78
Morris, Johnny 22,64,80
MotorGuide...77,118
mussels...2,4
National Bass Federation 76,80
night fishing 57,87,98
nitrogen 102,107,109
Nixa, Mo...9-10,110
noodling... see hand grabbing
Norfork...26,135
Novinger, Gary D. 67,69,89
Oasis... 24,32,43
OMC..117
Owen Boat Line..15,17,19
Owen, Jim...15-6,17,22
oxygen injection systems.........................118,134,140
oxygen, needed by bass 126
Ozark Ike 21
Ozark, Mo. 110
Ozarks Bass Club... 60
paddlefish snagging........................ 90-1,105-6,124,130
Patterson, Jim...88
pearls.. 4
Peck's Bait..16,17
pH meter 94
Philibert, Bob...5,23,24,30
phosphorus 102,107,110
phosphorus removal 110,139
pickerel...49
pitching technique..113
polarized glasses 96
Powersite..10,26,41
Predator props 95
public use areas 32-3

Radical 16,42
Ranger boats...............64,78,94,117
Rapala 19,56,60,73
record fish, paddlefish 130
record fish, striper...............133,136
record fish, white bass 132
Reeds Spring...............4,34
Reeves, Jim...............22,62
Richline boats 60,89
Roaring River 6,12-3,41,53,100
rock bass ....see goggle-eye
Rogers, Bill...............19
Rogue lure...............57,74
Ryck, Frank Jr...............55
scents 87,113-4
School of the Ozarks 14,60,75
Scott, Ray...............63,77,80
Secchi disk 107,111
Sequiota Creek...............56
Shell Knob 3,5,6,16,23,25,30,32,33,35,41
42,44,45,46,57,63,71,106,112
Sherfy, Duke 44,46
Shoreline Management Plan 33
Short, Dewey 27,40,42
sight fishing...............86,96
Silver Trol 60,77
Skeeter boats 78,94
Sloan, Stan 77
snagging ....see paddlefish
snowstorm phenomena 88
soft plastic jerkbait...............114
spearfishing...............54-5
split-shotting...............98,112,130
Sport Fish Restoration Act 96-7
Spring River...............55
stocking, paddlefish 65,90,91,106
stocking, threadfin shad 49,54,69

stocking, trout 13,52,53,129-30,138
stocking, walleye 49,53,54,65,91,129,138
stripers..133,136,138
structure fishing 71,81,131
Sucker Days..9-10
suckers 6,9-10,17,49
Sullivan, K.C 11-2,47,55
Symington, Senator Stuart 40,42
Table Rock Auxiliary Gated Spillway Project...................125,137
Table Rock Lake Water Quality, Inc..........................123
Table Rock Mountain 26
Table Rock Salvage Project.......................................31
Tarantula spinnerbait..81
Thomas, Dee 70
threadfin shad, compared to gizzard   shad...........................68-9
tie rafts... 3-4
Tilden, Buster 6,16-7
Tracker boats... 64
trot lines 5,17,22,51,52,60
trout, brook...130,138
trout, cutthroat..130,138
Upper White River Quality Project 123,126
Vance, Joel 106
Wallop-Breaux Amendment 97
Ward, Virgil..81,94
warmouth 121
water clarity, changes 110-1
Wiggle Wart 86,114,116
Wilderness Road 23,42
Wilson Creek...11,12,55
winter fishing..................66,88-9,96,98,106,120,131
wipers...122,133
Wood, Forrest...64
Woodwalker bait 72,79,100
Wright, Harold Bell 15
Y-bridge...25,42
Yelas, Jay 134

Yocum silver dollars 34
Yocum, Tom 19,20
Young, Fred 73
Zebco reels 19,21,56,60,84

Photo Credits

Photos courtesy Larry Bunch
cover catfish, pp. 6, 7, 18, 19, 20 (top), 24, 25 (top)

Photos courtesy J.D.Fletcher
pp. 8, 20 (bottom),62, 82 (top),121,122,136 (right)

Photos courtesy Shell Knob Chamber of Commerce
pp. 25 (bottom), 43, 45

Photos courtesy Eagle Rock Marina
pp. 82 (bottom),100 (top)

Photos courtesy Carl Garner
pp. 28, 37, 38, 39, 40

Photo courtesy Ed Garcia
p. 81

Photo courtesy Charlie Campbell
p. 100 (bottom)

Photo courtesy Jill Trimble
cover bridge

Charts courtesy Lakes of Missouri Volunteer Program
pp.108,109